LTHE DRAGON

Adventures in Chinese Media and Education

Abdiel LeRoy

Copyright 2017 Abdiel LeRoy

License Notes

This book is copyright material and must not be copied, reproduced, transferred, distributed, resold, licensed, or publicly performed except as permitted in writing by the author. Any unauthorized distribution or use of this text is an infringement of the author's rights.

ISBN
9781520746173

Cover illustration by Ignacio Pessolano

Books by Abdiel LeRoy

Non-fiction

The Gourmet Gospel: A Spiritual Path to Guilt-Free Eating

Dueling the Dragon: Adventures in Chinese Media and Education

Fiction

The Christmas Tree

Epic Poems

Obama's Dream: The Journey That Changed the World

Elijah: A Prophet's Tale

Poetry Collections

Verses Versus Empire: III — The Trump Era

Verses Versus Empire: II — The Obama Era

Verses Versus Empire: I — The George W. Bush Era

Well Versed: To Shakespeare, Poets, and the Performing Arts

What Others Are Saying About Dueling the Dragon

LeRoy's ability to write so cogently about such AWFUL things and simultaneously give readers a chuckle, is magnificent.

Peter Allemano

Wields a wicked and eloquent pen. I grow more horrified with each commentary. I will never, ever attempt to get a job in China. Period. This enlightened me to no end.

Steve Seiff

These stories from China are addictive.

Dixon Chen

Should be awarded an honorary degree in Anthropology. These accounts are an ethnographic study.

Andre Knights

These stories from China are always informative and eye-opening, and I read each one with fascination.

Richard Aven

This makes my neck hair stand on end and my tummy twitch. Hooorrrible! "Chinese law?" Yeah right! What exactly is that?

Christine Heike

To "Brother" Herman,
who has stood by me in my trials.

Table of Contents

Introduction ix

DUELING THE DRAGON

Dispatches From Chengdu   3

Laments From Leshan   67

Chidings From Changping   89

Briefings From Beijing   107

Perspectives From Peking   173

Closure   234

About the Author   236

Contact the Author   238

Footnotes   239

Introduction

Looking back over these chronicles, I tingle with embarrassment sometimes — at my naivety, overreactions, and missed opportunities. I even wonder what readers will infer about my psychological makeup at the time!

But rather than revise this book with the benefit of hindsight, I have favored giving voice to my former self as he was then. After all, *Dueling the Dragon* has its origins in a series of emails written to friends overseas, in which I was unfolding events more or less as they occurred. Nor have I seen a need to change anyone's name in these accounts.

I have also retained most of the original expletives, as they help to encapsulate my emotional responses at the time. I shun legalism in language as well as in life, and I am rather of Shakespeare's view that "there is nothing either good or bad but thinking makes it so."[1]

In any case, I trust readers will find the language less shocking than what it is responding to. I have witnessed universities complicit in honoring exam cheats, students sold into slavery while teachers pocket the proceeds, and farmers driven off their land by unscrupulous developers. My own direct experiences include false charges alleged by Beijing police, and persecution at China's state-media institutions. And I have not made any of this up!

Yet, from this nation of extremes, I also hope to offer some rays of light, including romantic encounters and moments of comedy. Which brings me to the central theme of the book — reflected in the title — that China is a nation of extreme contrasts. Though magical in all cultures, the Dragon is generally regarded as a benevolent being in China and as a malevolent one in the West. In my experience, the Chinese Dragon is fully both!

Dueling the Dragon is really five books in one, each covering a distinct period. The first, *Dispatches From Chengdu*, starts in 2005 with my early days as a teacher in the western province of Sichuan, followed by *Laments From Leshan*, a nearby city in the same province. My third teaching assignment is described in *Chidings From Changping*, a city near Beijing.

The fourth and fifth books, *Briefings From Beijing* and *Perspectives From Peking*, respectively, center around my experiences at Chinese state-media giants China Radio International, beginning in 2007, and China Central Television,[2] in 2015.

If you would like to hear my readings from this book, please visit the relevant Book page at poetprophet.com. You can hear excerpts from all my books at the site and join the guest list via the Contact page to get a free copy of my "little epic", *Obama's Dream*.

It is perhaps too much to hope that my observations about China will be prescriptive, but at least I can offer the perspective of an outsider, and sometimes it *takes* an outsider to observe the obvious!

In the end, if adventure stories contain both miracle and monster, friend and foe, then this book can justly claim to describe an adventure!

DUELING THE DRAGON

Dispatches From Chengdu

One

The floral designs on the sleeping bags seemed too pretty for military field equipment, but then again, the soldiers learning to fold them were far too lovely to be fighting any wars. I was on the campus of the Chengdu College of Film and Broadcasting, where squadrons of raven-haired beauties, clad in military camouflage, were undergoing their two weeks of compulsory military training before starting their first year at university.

Shy giggles, coy glances, and simple phrases of English greeted my declaration that "you're all doing very well!" And I was transported by their smiles alone. Were these fair damsels ever sent into battle, the mesmerized enemy would lay down their arms and raise up flags of a very different kind!

The girls here are dazzling, and I can imagine the Creator, when He fashioned the Eves of this world, must have looked with a particularly tender and gracious eye on Chengdu, which has earned the reputation, even among the Chinese, for its captivating examples of womanhood.

Speaking of Genesis, I am often charged with the sacred honor of naming the young adults around me, and have been assigning them names from Shakespeare, Scripture, mythology, and other great literature.

It's fun being an object of curiosity among the students here. Cries of "Hello!" welcome my daily walk across campus, usually followed by the pleasant harmony of giggles when I wave back with my own greeting.

Some of the girls say I'm handsome, reminding me of a line from, I think, *Mutiny on the Bounty*, where the island women think the English sailors "beautiful, no matter how oddly their features were arranged." Or, in the words of Shakespeare's *Richard III*: "Upon my life, she finds, though I cannot,/ Myself to be a marvelous proper man."[3]

But I have enjoyed hanging out with some of the lads too. One whom I have named James invited me to a "party" for the Moon Cake festival. It turned out to be a huge concert of theater, music, and dance. In response to their invitation that I should give a performance, I made up a solo Argentine-Tango dance, which was enthusiastically received.

The only words of English spoken during the evening were: "Long live Chairman Mao!" I find the ongoing reverence for Mao's memory hard to square with history but, if he had anything to do with putting first-year girls in military fatigues, I thank him!

Later, James told me, "my classmates very like you." I almost replied, "I very like them too!" In the end, I said something more grammatical, befitting an English teacher. Looking back, though, I like my first impulse better!

Two

"Today, I will buy you dumplings," said Alex. He felt it was his turn to pay after I bought him lunch last time.

This from an undergraduate who recently drowned his sorrows in several beers after his girlfriend's family rejected him as a future son-in-law, on the grounds of his own family's poverty. This from a man who, in all his four years at university, could afford only two trips home to his parents' farm in Xinjiang Province.

On his last visit — after a 56-hour train ride and three bus trips — his mother gave him the only mooncake she had, in celebration of China's Mid-Autumn Festival. Mooncakes are small pastries in the shape of hockey pucks, and they come with various fillings. Here in Chengdu, I received so many as gifts that I gave some away.

By comparison with most of my students, I am greatly privileged. I have my own apartment in the Foreign Teachers' Guesthouse. It has heating and air-conditioning, a phone, fridge, TV, and internet connection. There is a washing machine downstairs. And though the pay would bankrupt me in a week by New York standards, I am fed and clothed and housed reasonably comfortably.

But most of my charges at Chengdu University of Technology — or "CDUT" — live in conditions that would incite an uprising if tried in the West. The girls sleep eight to a dormitory, they must return before 11pm, and then make it through the remainder of the night without heating, air-conditioning, or even electricity! Showers are taken communally.

They also have to pay extra for hot water. The other day, I saw students paying an entrance fee to enter a tiled enclosure, where they filled tall flasks from a row of faucets lined against the wall. "What are they doing?" I asked. "Getting hot water," my friend replied. I then watched them walk off to their dorms, carrying these heavy burdens. One student badly scalded her leg the other day when her flask broke as she was walking.

I also recently visited the accommodations of some first-year boys, their limbs peppered with mosquito stings, and saw first-hand the conditions they live in — five guys with bunk-beds, sharing a very small room with a bare concrete floor, and close enough to the toilets that the smell of urine followed me in.

So when a student buys a teacher lunch, it is no small thing. In that one gesture is summarized the spirit of warmth and generosity I have found among the youngsters here. Furthermore, when I needed an answer machine, Alex searched doggedly through the shops of Chengdu, looking for the best deal. He then took me to the store, bargained a better price, set up the phone in my apartment, interpreted the instructions, and helped me to record my outgoing message.

Now he is helping me with installing a DVD player and fixing my computer, all of which he has volunteered without the smallest expectation in return. If ever there is a place in Heaven, make way for him! In the meantime, may Heaven answer with tender mercy Alex's question: "Does God think I don't need love?"

Three

Today, two of my students came up after class and showed me some lines of iambic poetry they had written. Had they merely written good English prose, the feat would have been astonishing enough.

In China, foreign visitors are relentlessly assaulted with bizarre arrangements of English words — symptomatic of a country growing faster than its competence. Among my favorites was a sign above a men's room saying "Toilet of Man". More recently, I came across this promotional copy from a bed manufacturer: "Whenever the time that night come, grow to have the Yalisi mattress sweet concomitant, let you fallen asleep safely in the quite night [*sic*]."

So for these two girls to be writing with Shakespeare's heartbeat within a few weeks of their first lesson plucks bright honor from the pale-faced moon![4] I could have kissed each one of them there and then!

Another encouragement: from time to time I have students tell of some difficult, shocking, or traumatic experience from their past, but using only the words of the nursery rhyme, *Hickory Dickory Dock*. It's an exercise I learnt in acting class. Today, deep called to deep[5] as one lad told his story, and we were moved to tears.

He was also wearing a character mask to tell the story, one of several I brought with me from the U.S. The mask's power to reveal the inner life accords with

Christ's observation that if a man will let himself be lost, he shall find his true self.[6]

I have also distributed small prizes, mostly postcard replicas of U.S. postage stamps celebrating the Chinese birth signs, for those who show unusual flair in the classroom. A couple of students have won bigger awards of Oscar Wilde poetry collections.

There is an element of stand-up comedy to my work here, though my Monty Python renditions were rather lost on them. And when I delivered the punchline of *The Three Sisters of Baghdad*, my favorite bawdy tale of *The Arabian Nights*, I was met with a surreal vista of blank faces.

Still, hearts are responding, and minds are catching up!

Four

"I haven't taken a deep breath since I came here!" So said one of the other foreign teachers here the other day. Understandable. Over the campus hovers a permanent chemical shadow, seeping into the lungs like liquid cancer, the effluent of seven great chimneys dominating the skyscape.

Belching their foul-tasting vapors day and night, they recall a dismal scene from Upton Sinclair's *The Jungle*: "thick, oily, and black as night...one stared, waiting to see it stop, but still the great streams rolled out...stretching a black pall as far as the eye could reach."

Here, the sun is seldom visible through the haze, and every leaf of every tree is coated with a grimy film. Near to the foreign teachers' building is a construction site — one of several on campus — banging and clanging day and night, adding the dust and exhaust fumes of delivery and cement trucks to the toxic pool.

And these chemical perils are almost matched by the biological ones. On the floors of most restaurants, strewn with food and phlegm spat out by shirtless men, sits a slippery film of grease where flies and roaches feast. Meat is stored without refrigeration in plastic bags under the counters.

Meanwhile, in the dark, fast-flowing river nearby, locals and students will take a dip on a hot day while all manner of filth floats by. I even saw the carcass of a dead pig making its way downstream! As for the public toilets, you don't even want me to go there. I certainly don't!

But my sensibilities here are not shared. Recently, when I recoiled in revulsion at a roach-sighting beside our hotpot at a local restaurant, the beautiful girl beside me calmly crushed the offending bug in a tissue, cast it to the floor, and got on with her meal.

What does cleanliness mean here anyway? Why, for instance, do I see workers hand-sweeping the nearby four-lane highway with long brooms while unwrapped pig carcasses trundle by on the backs of rusty mopeds?

Despite the questionable hygiene in eating establishments, I have enjoyed some delicious food in Chengdu, not just the "hotpot" for which the area is famous, but baked yams and roasted chestnuts bought on the street. My favorite place to eat is a Moslem restaurant near the campus front gate, where they serve a huge plate of lean beef with potatoes. It comes topped with cilantro which, I gather, is a good herb for detoxing!

Five

Child abuse comes in many forms. For Bond, one of my Chinese student friends here on campus, it was attempted strangulation by his mother when he was six months old. Catching her in the act, his father placed him in the care of Bond's paternal grandmother, who lived in the same remote village. Even so, his mother would beat Bond if she came across him outside.

Following divorce between Bond's parents, his father resolved never to marry again, for fear of what a stepmother might inflict on the boy and his younger brother.

Like many childhood traumas, details are patchy, and the motivations unfathomable. But they are part of an abusive pattern recounted by many students here, including deliberate starvations, tying up children to be left unattended, jabbing with sharp objects, and sexual exploitation.

Nor are China's education policies helping. I was shocked to learn that Chinese families have to pay for their children's education. What?! A self-declared Communist country is charging its kids to go to school? When I was growing up in England, every child could go free-of-charge to a "comprehensive" school, though England never declared itself a Communist country.

And when I went to university, the government not only paid for my tuition but supplied a modest grant to help with living expenses and supplies. What brand of

Communism denies its people the right to benefits other non-Communist countries provide?

Add to that the large gender imbalance of the population, with many more boys than girls in graduating age groups, resulting from China's one-child-per-family policy, and it quickly becomes clear that the country's sociological problems run very deep. The other day, a young man at this university jumped to his death from a campus building after his girlfriend broke up with him. I am told that suicides are quite frequent here and that suicide is the country's number-one killer of young people.

Six

Getting up early is so much easier here. Knowing my "commute" is but a short walk across campus, and that my fellow travelers are students on their way to class, I do not experience the dread that preceded early starts in New York City or London, the crush of bodies in confined spaces, and the grey, resentful faces resigned to a miserable routine.

The facilities here are poor, and so is the pay, nor is the university high on the academic pecking order, but I count myself blessed to be doing something rewarding and happy. I am igniting a passion for learning among my students and watching with delight as it fans into flame.[7] This week, in response to their homework assignment to memorize four lines of English poetry, four girls together recited by turns Shakespeare's cuckoo song from *Love's Labour's Lost*.

And so many beauties among them. If my friends could see me now!

Among my favorite moments are the "punishments" I mete out for minor infractions, such as cellphones going off or arriving late. I bring the student to the front of the room where they can choose to do a silly face or a silly walk. And if the response is not sufficiently silly, I will clown their shy gestures and faces, which greatly amuses the remainder.

There is a wonderful energy among the students at the "broadcast college" campus, where I conduct about half my classes. Once a week, the school sends a car to ferry me there, when I get to see some rather more rural settings than those surrounding the parent university. The most ubiquitous vehicles are tricycles, some motorized but most not, usually carrying fruit or vegetables. Outside the campus are rows of little shops and eateries.

What corporate job can compare to this?

Seven

Of all men the drunkard is the foulest. The thief when he is not stealing is like another. The extortioner does not practise in the home. The murderer when he is at home can wash his hands. But the drunkard stinks and vomits in his own bed and dissolves his organs in alcohol.

Ernest Hemingway, For Whom The Bell Tolls

As those...
Who never tasted wine will value beer
Too highly, so the smut-hound, since he knows
Neither God, hunger, thought, nor battle, must
Of course hold disproportioned views on lust.

C.S. Lewis, the poem ODORA CANUM VIS

There are a kind of people among whom beer is a social currency. I've never liked it, but beer is the lubricant of choice among many of the foreign teachers here, a largely Australian contingent. Along with drinking at all hours in the neighboring flats, they play loud music and sustain a nightly cacophony of shouting, slamming, and banging.

Moreover, my polite requests they be aware others are trying to sleep are met with such witty ripostes as "get fucked" or "don't accuse me of being a fucking criminal!"

Meanwhile, I've found closer community with the North American foreign teachers: Don, who has helped me to adjust to life in China; Henry, who has turned out to be a dedicated and faithful yoga partner; Vivian, who has been a good neighbor with her practical helps; and Mary, who came to my room with earplugs on learning of my distress about lack of sleep.

It was a kind gesture, though I already have earplugs and they are but poor defense against the noisy assaults of other occupants in this reverberate building.

The unreliable internet connection here, the frequent power blackouts, the occasional lack of hot water, and inadequate laundry facilities I can deal with, but to Hell with this brotherhood of beer!

Eight

This week, I got a call from the university administration. Apparently, some students in one of my classes complained it was too hard for them to memorize English poetry for homework. And now the administration is calling on me to set "easier tasks."

Bollocks! Mnemosyne, the goddess of Memory, is mother of all the muses, and I am helping students to build a treasury of the mind. Furthermore, most of my students have already handed me their lists of memorized verse.

I told the administration I would consider their request, but find I can not agree to this. After sharing my response with the class, I received a couple of e-mails from them (unedited):

"In my opinion, although I'm not always understand you meanings, I like making me busy and enrich. And I think we will learn more from you. so I think we should thank you, you give another world, and you did very well.
"Bonnie."

"I hope you won't be sad of what the administrant said to you. As you say that's not the majority's point. Simon and I both think you are a very good teacher, and you have strong responsibility to all of us. Your enthusiasm, humor, profoundness and kindness attract us so much.

*"One more thing I want to thank you is that I can recite two sonnets now (actually I can recite them two weeks ago). All of this is from your efforts. And Simon will bring you a tape, hoping you can read some sonnets to us. Thank you once again.
"Sarah."*

Nine

Chinese is a fiendishly difficult language. Not only do otherwise identical syllables have completely different meanings according to which of the four "tones" are used in pronouncing them, but even identical syllables with identical tones can have different meanings too!

Reading, of course, is even harder, because it means identifying Chinese characters, of which there are tens of thousands, the vast majority a blurry mass of tiny squiggles that swim before my eyes in dizzying confusion. China has developed a set of "simple" characters as an alternative to the "complex" ones still used in Taiwan, but really the choice is between "complex" and "more complex".

Nevertheless, I am making progress with reading some Chinese poetry, assisted by a fourth-year student, Hazel, who records it on to tape, translates the Chinese characters into Pinyin — a transcription system that uses letters of the Western alphabet — and helps me to understand their meaning.

I met her on a bus that ferries students and teachers between campus and the nearby Carrefour shopping center. She is one of several students who have come to my rescue when I needed to buy things, although the reply from shopkeepers is usually the same: "méiyǒu," literally meaning "not have."

Ten

Like Tennyson's Maud, Jennifer is "tall and stately." From Xinjiang Province in the north of China, she stands out from the shorter local girls of Chengdu. And she has brains to match her beauty, loving as she does works of English literature I count among my favorites, such as *Wind in the Willows* or Oscar Wilde's *The Nightingale and the Rose*.

I met her at English Corner, where dozens of eager students form clusters around a few foreign teachers and ask about anything and everything. I especially enjoyed the following conversation with one of the girls.

Student: "Do you have a girlfriend?"
Me: "No, no girlfriend."
Student: "Do you like babies?"

We had a good laugh about that. The night I met Jennifer, it started to rain, and she shared an umbrella with me as we carried my teaching materials back.

Alas, she has a boyfriend, but there was compensation a few days later, when she visited with four of her dorm-mates. They are an example of those loving sisterhoods Chinese girls form with each other. I often see them walking hand-in-hand across campus in lines of two, three, four, or even five.

The familial bonds established between students, among the boys too, is apparent from the terms of affection used: "mèimei" (little sister), "jiějie" (big sister), "dìdi" (little brother), and "gēge" (big brother). My dear friend Alex, now in his fourth and final year, is known as "dà shū," meaning "Big Uncle," for his capacity in caring for others.

Finding a partner tall enough for Argentine Tango was a challenge, but last week I spied a lovely girl near the north campus who is a perfect height. I named her Helen, and our first practice session was very encouraging. Also ranking among the towering graces is the stunning Sharon from Shanghai.

As for my student, Joanna, I had glimpsed her beauty but vaguely until she invited me to her group dance performance, in which she was wearing a boob top and skin-tight stretchpants. Now she is my partner for Jive dancing.

Catherine is another cutie, her radiant smile alternating with looks of bemusement, head tilted to one side, as she ponders something. In the words of Charles Dickens: "The changing expression of sweetness and good humour, the thousand lights that played about her face, and left no shadow there; above all, the smile, the cheerful, happy smile, were made for Home, and fireside peace and happiness."[8]

I met Nicole, who attends another university in Chengdu, while she was running a coffee stand near the city center, and we have got together a few times since. Adding to the allure of her gorgeous raven-black hair is the natural pout of her lips.

Beauty runs especially deep at the broadcast college. Gina, with her large eyes and dimpled cheeks, is breathtaking; the tall Emily, with her angular and striking features, a dream; and another Catherine, her eyes like almonds in a sea of milk, a sculptor's desire.

Here is beauty in infinite variety.

Eleven

I had an in-the-zone teaching moment today. I wrote some lines of verse on the blackboard and asked the students what the rhythm was. No answer. "Rhythm?" I asked. "You know what that word means?" No answer.

"Ok," I explained. "In music, you have a melody, a tune, like …"

I started to hum Beethoven's *Ode to Joy*. They joined in.

Then I sang the opening notes of Beethoven's Fifth. Again, they joined in. "OK," I said. "This music has a rhythm," which I then proceeded to clap out.

"Now. Do you recognize this rhythm?" I asked, clapping out the opening to *Eine Kleine Nachtmusik* without the melody.

They got it, and began humming the tune from merely hearing the beat.

This prepared the ground to introduce the heartbeat — iambic — rhythm in English verse.

We went on to sing "London's Burning" in a four-part round.

Twelve

Even though it is now mid-November, mosquitoes still swarm on the campus, and lately I have been awoken in the middle of the night by their stings, in spite of my best efforts with insect repellent and vapor devices.

Last night, one got me at 4am, and there was no point trying to sleep again, because I had to be up at 5.30 anyway for a whole day of teaching at the broadcast college.

But the car never showed up. I called the assistant, who told me I was not teaching there any more. I checked my e-mail. There was a message from a student, sent the previous day, asking why I was no longer teaching them! So the students knew before I did!

All my preparatory labors were wasted — planning class content, assembling materials for the day, e-mailing files to the students, updating student contact information and assessments, recording tapes of poetry and literature for students who had requested them, reworking poetry some had written, and agonizing about how to deal with one student who had been trying to disrupt class.

On top of that, I had printed great quantities of handouts at my own expense, collated them, and stapled them, because the university does not provide printers for the students to use on campus, and the administration had earlier complained about the amount of ink used in printing out my previous materials!

So all I have invested, all that groundbreaking work to lay the foundations of inspiration, are for naught. And I had prepared so much more to give as well. Yet the assistant informed me that such behavior is "normal at our university."

The only upside to this debacle is that I can now get better rest. The extra hours at CDUT's sister broadcasting college not only exceeded the contractual maximum, but required two road trips a week, each leg lasting up to an hour and half.

I had tried staying at the broadcast college one night per week to cut down on the traveling, but was put in a noisy concrete cell, complete with steel door and barred peephole, with neither heat for cold nights nor air-conditioning for hot ones, a bunk bed that was too short, bed linen that stank of mold, a hole in the floor for a toilet, and, to top it all, swarming with mosquitoes! I got one hour of very uncomfortable sleep that night before disco music started blaring from the campus radio station at 6.30 in the morning!

I still have my students at the main campus, but now I have lost the group with whom I felt the closest affinity. I managed to send an e-mail to most of them explaining I had not abandoned them and that my absence was due to circumstances beyond my control.

And the response has been extremely supportive, with messages from at least 16 students, some of which I reproduce below:

"I am crying now. I am very sad that you can not teach us in the future. I like you and I will always miss you."

"We all miss you very much, and we hope you can keep touch with us as well. We are friends, nothing can change it. God bless us."

"Today I heard the news you would not teach us any more? I was so puzzled. We all thought your teaching was so good, and we have learned so much about Shakespeare."

"I'm very disappointed to get this news. Everyone knows that you a good teacher, and the college cheats us. But you know, the college can't stop us missing you."

"Last Thursday, when we heard the news, we were all shocked! We all still think that you are a crackerjack teacher! Thank you what you have done for us!!!"

"All of us are missing you, hope you can come back to teach us, we do not understand the actions of our school."

"Thanks for teaching me, I won't forget you in the future. You are a very kind person. What a pity that you can't teach me. All of the students love you very much. Best wishes to you! I am your student forever!"

"I didn't know how to say my feeling. Of course, so sad. I like your class. And now, I mostly don't go to class any more. You are the best teacher in my opinion. I can't believe our university will do this."

"I am so confused with what our school did to you!!!!! It was unfair. What happened??? We all like you very much, you are humorous, handsome, did a lot for us. We all know that you love us very much, and we love you so much, still remember the silly dancing, silly singing, it still can touch my heart when I think of you."

"We are glad you were our teacher. We can learn lots of things that are very important and useful to us. For example, learning foreign culture, seeing great films, dancing, and so on. We all think you are a great teacher."

"When I see the materials that you give us, I am very touched. You still consider us your students. From these things, I can see you are very responsible teacher, which is very rare."

Damn this college administration for their stupidity, blindness, and ignorance!

Thirteen

Today at lunch, I was introduced to a girl who is about to graduate in English after four years at university. Yet she could not understand even my simplest and slowest sentences! What is wrong with the education system in this country that is outwardly so hungry to improve the English skills of its populace while it accommodates students like this?

And in a textbook shown me by a second-year English major, the chapter headings alone — such as "Past Participle Predicatives", "Sentences of Unreal Condition", and "The Present Participle as Attributive Modifier" — are enough to put anyone off learning English for life! "Sharp of eye, yet how dull of vision!" to quote the famed actress Ellen Terry when she was talking about critics.

I have also learned from conversations with students how, by imposing relentless batteries of tests on children from an early age, the system stifles rather than stimulates discovery.

But it just got worse! Earlier this week, the head of the Foreign Language Department called in seven of us foreign teachers for a meeting. Even while he was encouraging us to talk about Western culture, he instructed us not to use the Bible in our classes!

Bollocks again! The Bible is a key foundation of our language — a treasury of poem, parable, and prophecy — AND of our culture! Can he really be that stupid? Give me a break!

Fourteen

Of 12 contestants, maybe three could hold a tune. And only one was truly gifted.

But she did not win the *English Song Competition* that I was helping to host at CDUT. Instead, the prize went to a denizen of discord who would do better to confine his misplaced melodies to karaoke rooms peopled with long-suffering friends practiced in the art of unconditional love, than to amplify his artlessness to a packed auditorium!

Tuneless, talentless, and tempo-less, the contestants shrieked, wailed, and warbled through rock songs, murdering such classics as *Hey Jude*, and deeply offending the memory of The Carpenters.

The entrants were beyond bad, excruciatingly, shockingly awful — off-key, off-kilter, off-scale — yet oblivious to their own inadequacies.

Where's a shitometer when you need one?!

Fifteen

I could not kiss her enough. I adored her.

"You love me more, because you kiss me more!" she said teasingly as we embraced. And we both laughed as I hugged her again. I was squatting down to be at her level, and I kissed her again on the cheek several times in rapid succession.

Then I stood up, lifting her off the ground with me, and holding her tightly in my arms. I wept. For she was leaving, with her mother. And I felt the pangs of losing them both as I set her down again and they started to go. "How can I love so completely this little girl?" I asked myself, as I watched them depart.

I awoke to find my eyes wet with the subconscious tears that had spilled into the waking world.

I know the mother, and this is the second time I have dreamed about her this week. She is Yan, my ex, now living in New York. Perhaps the little girl represents the future we will not have.

Sixteen

Ungrateful bastards! Some in the postgraduate class are complaining that I'm treating them like children because I have them occasionally put on theatrical masks. They say they are not actors, that they feel embarrassed, that this is not in their "culture", yet howl in protest when I assign them a low score on class participation as a result.

I have come to China, to the other side of the world, an enormous risk. Yet I encounter some students here who are not even willing to venture a toe in the water with this new experience! It's sad, and pathetic. And it's a lie. Chinese culture embraces the theatrical mask at least as much as Western culture!

What a stark contrast with the ebullience and joy that surged from the first-year students at the broadcast college. Were these postgrads similarly enthused when they set out on their university education? And did the college system snuff out every spark of curiosity amid this "dross of indifference"?[9]

Thus my good seed falls in rocky places, among hearts of stone, among the thorns of denial,[10] even of learning more about themselves. I am unequally yoked.[11] Why cast my pearls before these swine?[12]

Seventeen

There is an ill wind blowing through that postgraduate class. "Poets are crazy!" one of them asserted when about to undertake her assignment of reciting a poem.

"I give that back to you," I replied. "I didn't ask you to comment about the poem, just to recite it."

Then she upped the ante in the next class. "We don't like poetry!" she declared.

Now, I can deal with someone saying, "*I* don't like poetry." You're missing out, but hey, that's up to you. It's the presumption of speaking for the rest of the class that I find so galling.

I had her rephrase the statement: "*I* do not like poetry."

"So do you like prose?" I asked, thinking I could adjust her assignment to recite prose instead.

"No!" she answered.

"So you don't like prose and you don't like poetry. That means you don't like language. Why have you devoted six years of your life to a subject you don't like?"

No answer.

A week of anxiety, torment, and prayer, wrestling with what to do about this student, how to "guard my heart with all diligence."[13]

"Here's a metaphor," I began the following week. "Anyone heard of the phrase 'bad apple'?"

And it went downhill from there, with the student in question slamming her fist down on the desk and declaring, "China is a free country!"

This episode resulted in some earnest conversations with the university's HR office and an agreement that I and this postgraduate class would part company after the semester.

Eighteen

I stifled my laugh as Cindy handed in her exam paper. The time limit had not yet expired, and other students in this undergraduate class were still at work. Besides, I didn't want anyone to interpret my merriment as laughing *at* Cindy, instead of *with* her.

The question was: "Why does the English language have such a rich vocabulary?" I was looking for an answer outlining its Latin and Germanic roots. But I had to give Cindy a point for sheer audacious flattery:

"Because of Englishmen's great wisdom," she wrote.

Among the other amusing responses to this question, a couple of candidates attributed the richness of vocabulary to the 26 letters of the alphabet. Nice try!

In answers to other questions, the parents of the Muses (Zeus and Mnemosyne) were described as "their father and mother"; two sons of Priam were "Paris and his brother"; and the angel that leads the rebellion against God in *Paradise Lost* was "Santa."

Upon reflection, I gave half marks for that answer. After all, it is an anagram of the correct one, and the devil does masquerade as an angel of righteousness.[14] And doesn't Santa's list-keeping of "whose been naughty or nice" smack of devilish legalism?

Fair play to my students!

Nineteen

I remember an episode from my school days in which I copied my neighbor's test answers, thinking him better informed than I was. Usually, that was the case; he was known as the class "swot". But on this occasion, my trust was misplaced, for he had not prepared any better than I.

The following week, the teacher, noticing we had the same wrong answers, wrote "COPY!" on our papers. A number of other pairs of students had received the same comment. Well, I guess that sort of thing goes on among 10-year-olds.

But among postgraduate students? It is one in the morning, and I am so stunned by what I have just seen in these final exam papers, that I am unable to sleep. I was not overseeing the exam itself, so I don't know how they communicated with each other, but the patterns of identical incorrect answers, identical incorrect spellings, and identical answers to open-ended questions leave no doubt that cheating was rife. They even suggest connivance by the invigilating teacher!

I was at first pleasantly surprised by the answers of one girl whose work during the semester had been especially uninspiring. But now I know she was leaning on a more accomplished student, and wasn't even smart enough to disguise what she had been up to!

And this from a group of students who complained I treated them like children! Turns out I credited them with more maturity than they deserve! I have assigned zero scores to the definite cheaters while giving the benefit of the doubt to the ones I merely suspect.

Yet the university administration has instructed me to group the majority of percentage scores for this class in the 80s for the semester!

I'm told by Chinese friends that cheating is rife in the Chinese education system, that students sometimes pay great sums to have exam answers fed to them via text messages or tiny earphones, and some will even appoint a substitute to sit for them under a false identity. My dearest friend Alex informs me he has turned down several lucrative offers to serve as an exam proxy. Even scholarships are won illicitly, he tells me, meaning that "the people who really need them don't get them."

Of course, all this means that candidates are leaving college to build careers on a foundation of sand. I heard the other day that multinational corporations in China find only 10% of the country's university graduates have English skills adequate to work for them. Having observed so many getting certification beyond their accomplishments, I am not surprised!

Twenty

And so to my first Christmas in China. I spent the day with dear friends Alex and Sharon, first at a potluck lunch put together by the foreign teachers then at a Peking duck restaurant for dinner with another Chinese friend, Vivien.

Alex has been a godsend, an entertaining companion who reflects both the poetic and the profane English he has heard from me!

Tomorrow, we're off to another restaurant for a Western-style Christmas dinner with my pretty friend, Nicole. Last week, I accepted an invitation to guest teach at her English class at another university in Chengdu. I talked about Christmas in England and shared a brief excerpt from my *Wind in the Willows* one-man show.

I have received some very thoughtful gifts and messages from students, too. Phoebe gave me a mask of the Monkey King from the famous Chinese tale, *Journey to the West*. In her card, she wrote:

> *You arrived in Chengdu, met us, and then became our foreign teacher. I regard it as my honour to be your student.*
>
> *It's you who have shown me the beauty of English and English poems, which I never found before. You have really opened a door for me to the fascinating English world.*

At this moment, I want to show you my gratitude by this little card and say 'Thank you!' from the bottom of my heart.

Another student presented me with a gorgeous painting from Yunnan Province, and two others gave me scarves they had knitted by hand!

At the close of Christmas Day, I enjoyed a delicious Christmas cake made by one of the foreign teachers. He and I have not been on speaking terms for much of the semester, but I shall write him a thank-you note now. Peace and Goodwill to all men, and all of that.

Twenty-One

It's called "guānxi" — meaning "connection" or "relationship," but often used as a euphemism for graft and corruption. Today, having spent a couple of hours in the Chengdu customs office filling out forms and listening to Alex wrestle with the bureaucracy in Chinese, I came face-to-face with it.

The officials have levied an "administrative fee" for me to get my FedEx package. It entitles me to come back the following day to pick up some papers, so that I can take them away and get them stamped and bring them back. Then I must deliver those papers to FedEx myself, so that FedEx can move my package from the customs office in the southern city of Shenzhen.

I looked at the staff in this office. They're all supposed to speak English, but none do. Rather, these guānxi-drenched individuals devote their days to reading newspapers, playing computer games, smoking, and chatting.

And when I returned to pick up the papers the following day — after another hour-long bus ride — they said they weren't ready because they'd had a meeting that day. Try again tomorrow. I checked my package status online. For several days now, it has read: "Regulatory agency clearance delay." No shit!

Finally, after three visits to the customs office, I received the sacred document, handed over another fee, and watched the official put it straight in his pocket! Another week has since gone by, and still no word on the status or delivery date.

Twenty-Two

My recent hassles with Chinese customs recall my struggles even getting here in the first place. It began with missing my connection in Beijing, because the Air China flight left Kennedy Airport two hours late. So I had to spend the night in Beijing.

And so did all my luggage. Having dragged it all to the Air China desk, they would not let me check it in for the next day's flight. I was turned away from one overnight storage facility at the airport because they were closing, but managed to find another still open, which I would have to pay for myself.

As I was trying to get my stuff through their x-ray machine, some Chinese people decided they would push in front.

"Fuck!" I cried out.

It seemed to do the trick, and I finally got my stuff stowed. After a taxi ride, I was allotted to a hotel room that I had to share with a stranger. The following day, despite the absence of a scheduled wake-up call, I made it back to the airport and retrieved my luggage.

I returned to the Air China counter, where they attempted to levy against me another excess baggage fee for the remainder of my journey to Chengdu, on top of the fee I had already paid in New York. Only the intervention of a supervisor averted this additional costly blow.

Some friends have dubbed me an "international man of mystery," but the reality's not as glamorous as it sounds!

Twenty-Three

The university has decided to fire me. They accuse me of teaching "religion" and of being unsatisfactory according to teachers at the broadcast college. And they are proposing to do this without meeting their obligations in the contract, first to issue a warning and also to pay a breach fee.

Meanwhile, students at the broadcast college inform me they are refusing to continue their classes with the teachers brought in to replace me. Popular with the students; unpopular with the teachers? I wonder why!

But all of this is very old news, anyway. It is the timing of the administration's move that is perhaps most telling, coming one day after I sent in the postgraduate student scores.

Twenty-Four

*But how I caught it, found it, or came by it,
What stuff 'tis made of, whereof it is born,
I am to learn.*

William Shakespeare, *Merchant of Venice*

I know not where or when I contracted it, or from whom. But whatever the source, I clearly didn't take sufficient precautions, and I am now paying for it with a nasty infection!

I thought I would get away with it, that it couldn't happen to me, that this is the sort of thing that only happens to other people, and that somehow I was cloaked with divine protection against my own errings. Not so!

But lest you jump to the wrong conclusion, the affliction of which I speak is worms. And they fell out in an unholy cluster yesterday!

I had been experiencing digestion problems for some time. Now I know why!

Twenty-Five

I love the Shakespeare Insult Kit. I have seen it release great joy, exuberance, energy, and enthusiasm among those who play with it. Comprising two columns of adjectives and one of nouns, all taken from the plays of Shakespeare, it provides the building blocks for some spectacularly clever put-downs, especially with alliterative constructions: "You Fawning, Fen-sucked, Footlicker!" for example, or "You Misbegotten, Milk-livered, Maggot-Pie!"

So imagine my surprise when this seditious text was brought in as evidence against me by school administrators! They also complained that I had taught about "religion" and "sex". I don't know if it was my reference to the Bible as a foundation of the English language, or to its treasure-house of metaphor, or to the double-meanings in the Song of Solomon. But somebody seemed to sniff subversion in there somewhere!

Still, some forms of religion are permitted, it seems. "The students are God," the presiding professor told me. "They pay your salary and mine."

This use of my own teaching materials as prosecutorial exhibits also lends an ironic twist, given that I had printed them all at my own expense and inconvenience. I suppose it serves me right for declining the administration's earlier suggestion that I pass the hat around among my students to cover such costs!

One final accusation: "You were eight minutes late to one of your classes."

I have never been late for a single class, so I asked, "Really? Which day was that?"

"Oh, I don't have that information," he replied.

No matter how much experience I have in this world, I am still shocked by its lies, fabrications, straining of gnats,[15] and calling good "evil".[16] Its schemers are of that ilk that would condemn the healing of a crippled man because it happened on the Sabbath![17]

In the end, my reminder that they would have to pay a breach-of-contract penalty for firing me seemed to do the trick. And I am engaged for a second semester!

Twenty-Six

I am as Elijah sitting under his tree in the desert after Jezebel's death threat,[18] paralyzed with depression and loneliness. Most of the students have left, or are about to leave, for the long Winter vacation. They walk in droves to the front gate to catch buses and taxis, and the campus is becoming increasingly deserted.

Yet still the melancholy period bell rings across campus at preset times to tell of classes that are not happening. I ask not for whom it tolls...

I dread the next semester. I am still licking my wounds from the first. I don't know if I can face it again. I don't know how I will cope if the same situations and difficulties resurface.

I have begun reading *There Are No Shortcuts*, a book by U.S. inner-city teacher Rafe Esquith. In his opening paragraph, he writes: "Those of us who have survived school have plenty of scars. Any person who has taught for more than a few years has met administrators, teachers, parents, and children who, as Mark Twain once remarked, 'make a body ashamed of the human race.' "

Esquith goes on to warn:

> *Ignorance and mediocrity are forever busy, and the forces of mediocrity aren't content with being mediocre; they'll do everything in their power to prevent even the humblest of teachers and children from accomplishing anything extraordinary... If you care about your profession, if you dare to be*

different in any way, and if you have the courage to aim for real excellence, these negative forces will eventually marshal themselves against you... So be prepared for battle, unless you want to be like everyone else.

He does offer a message of hope, however, "that you can have success as a teacher despite the many forces that are working against you." And his advice to "choose material you personally love" certainly resonates with me.

Still, I keep hoping for an acting or publishing offer I can't refuse to whisk me back to the States so that I don't have to face the next semester!

Twenty-Seven

"What the guests see looks very, very clean, but in the basement it is very, very dirty."

So Bond describes conditions at the Chengdu hotel where he works every night until two in the morning, or even four, although they only pay him to one o'clock. He carries beer and liquor to patrons and prostitutes in the hotel's karaoke bar — for which he is paid 50 dollars a month — in order to satisfy credits required by the university for his graduation.

This he must do because his parents are poor farmers without the guānxi to get him a falsified credit for work experience or the funds to pay off his teachers.

After his shift, Bond returns to the filthy dormitory he shares with five unwashed, chain-smoking colleagues, lies down on a bare steel frame with a cardboard mattress, and tries to sleep. One of his fellow workers has smuggled a TV into the room, where it is covered with cardboard and a tablecloth in order to appear like a table — this because hotel management has banned TVs in workers' rooms as a waste of electricity!

In any case, Bond has little interest in the TV shows favored by his colleagues, preferring to use what little spare time he has for reading and studying, and in teaching English to other members of the hotel and kitchen staff. He is one of the most diligent and humble men I have ever met, his soul athirst for learning and truth.

Meanwhile, he shuns the exam cheating that prevails among his fellow students, even though it means enduring their derision.

It is not my place to say who shall ascend to Heaven,[19] but I venture to nominate Bond as an inheritor of blessed eternity. Meanwhile, he has five more months of squalor to look forward to!

Twenty-Eight

Censorship is alive and well in China. On first arriving, I had been frustrated in my efforts to use a Bible concordance website. But the site had been unreliable even in the U.S., so I found another one and didn't pay much attention.

But now this second website, which I had been using without any problem for months, has suddenly become inaccessible.

Earlier this week, I heard a report on *Democracy Now*, entitled *The Great Firewall of China*, which examines how the Chinese government is restricting its citizens' internet search results and access to websites, with the cooperation of Google, Yahoo, and Microsoft.

The most egregious conspirator so far has been Yahoo, who identified someone who posted a government document online, and this led to the person's sentencing to 10 years' hard labor!

I tried to save the broadcast transcript, but every attempt got me locked out of the entire website.

Meanwhile, the Chinese government has produced a paper about introducing democracy into its processes provided, of course, that the Communist Party stays in power!

Twenty-Nine

I have had metaphorical monkeys on my back in the past. But this was my first literal experience. And I must have presented quite a spectacle as I span around trying to dislodge the tenacious primate by centrifuge.

Moments before, my friend had been charged by a particularly ferocious specimen, the size of a pit bull terrier, fast, muscular, and agile, that suddenly darted from nearby foliage like furred fury.

We were on the famed Emei Mountain, which is about 2-1/2 hours from Chengdu by bus. And these were our first encounters with its privileged primates.

Two things interest this troop: food and sex, often at the same time. We had bought sachets of special food to "feed the monkeys," but the beneficiaries had no intention of seeking by entreaty what could be had by command.

"I was indecently assaulted by a monkey," wrote one tourist, "but they will use contraception if asked politely." This comment was one of hundreds on the lobby walls of the Teddy Bear Hotel, a kind of magnet for foreign tourists among the many hotels at the foot of the mountain.

For me, the chief attraction of this hotel is its Western-style breakfast, followed by the entertainment value of reading the walls. "Quel domage que le temps soit si 'British,' " commented a former French visitor. ("What a shame the weather is so 'British.' ")

Most of the time we were there, the summit was swathed in cloud. Still, the opportunity of breathing all that fresh air and sitting in a pool fed by hot springs was more than enough compensation.

Other than scribblings on the hotel walls, there are no official warnings about the monkeys. However, a band of vigilant women are stationed at the key trouble spot — armed with sticks, stones, and catapults — to deter the most egregious offenses. Some useful advice might have been: conceal all food and drink, keep hands open (because a clenched hand suggests food), carry a stick, and if attacked pretend to throw a stone. But then again, such suggestions might have spoiled the surprise!

If only my postgraduate students had come with such warnings!

Thirty

If I remember correctly, the word "serendipity" means something like "a lucky mistake". With that in mind, I welcome the fortuitous homonym in an e-mail just received from a former student at the broadcast college.

When she returns from the Winter vacation, she writes, "I will bring my hometown's pair to you. It is the best famous fruit of our city. I look forward to backing too..."

And I look forward to fronting!

Thirty-One

I was getting into my flow with this new class of students in the second semester, when I suddenly noticed an older participant seated in the back corner. She seemed not to be paying much attention and was busy writing something.
    I walked toward her.
    "Hello," I said.
    "Hello," she answered. "I am the teacher for this class."
    Funny. I thought I was!
    I am charged with teaching more than 1,500 students this semester, with each group receiving a class once every three weeks. And their Chinese teachers can drop in whenever they feel like it. I must make bricks without straw[20] and, moreover, do so under the closest scrutiny!
    The other foreign teachers have been allocated a similar patchwork timetable, prompting speculation this is to tell students and parents that they are getting tuition from a foreign teacher, however thinly we are spread!
    My aim for the coming months is to enjoy myself and not take any of this stuff too seriously.

Thirty-Two

In my schoolboy days, we all feared Timothy Vallis on the cricket pitch. His bowling was wickedly fast, coming at you in a blur of red rage. A bowler doesn't just stand and throw, like a baseball pitcher, but may take as long a run-up as he likes, and work up as much speed as he likes, before windmilling his arm down and unleashing fury.

But I knew, when my turn came to face him, that there was no point in cowering before his speed. That would have left me even more vulnerable. So I attacked his incoming salvo with unflinching aggression. And having struck the ball with my bat, what a glorious feeling to see it sailing back over his head to the boundary!

Now, I revisit this boyhood metaphor in my mind, realizing I need to face the next semester with similar resolve.

With a few classes under my belt, I am beginning to enjoy myself again, beginning to look forward to meeting each new group and having a laugh with them. One advantage of teaching so many different sets of students is that I can use the same material over and over again.

Not that I get bored because, like an actor playing the same role on successive nights, I still have room for variation and spontaneity each time.

"You're cut out to be a teacher," one of the students here told me. I'm starting to believe it again.

Thirty-Three

Today, I talked with Jane, one of my top students from last semester at the broadcast college. She is in considerable distress about how poorly they are being instructed in English.

They have no foreign teachers now, and most of their tuition comes from other undergraduates who do not have a strong sense of their responsibility, do not prepare adequately for classes, and talk mostly in Chinese. Many of their classes are taken up watching TV shows and movies they have not discussed beforehand.

The school is also refusing to divide the class from its current size of more than 50 students. To cap it all, they are paying dearly for this poor education.

Jane worries, and rightly so, that she is being inadequately prepared for her future career, but her lobbying efforts to bring improvement, supported by other leading students of the class, have fallen on deaf ears with the school's administration.

I told her by way of encouragement, that with her determination and hunger for learning, she will find her place and success with or without the university's help. In the meantime, I wonder into whose pockets those 50 tuition fees are going!

Thirty-Four

Forget pole dancing, belly dancing, or any of the other gyrations that have stoked the desires of men. The Peacock Dance — "kǒngquè wǔ" — originating from Yunnan Province, is in a whole other league of sexiness.

Most of the time, the dancer's back was turned to the audience, whence the roundness of her buttocks, stirring in the red shimmer of her dress, brought every hormone to the boil. Oh, to be held in the bedroom by what I *be*held on stage!

Thirty-Five

Having declined the Shakespearean names I suggested, she still calls herself "Wing." And why not? For she stirs a man to flights of fancy. Her high cheekbones are a supermodel's envy, her height a towering summons, and those gorgeous long legs a universal head-turner.

Although this 21-year-old daily adorns herself with short skirts, high heels and makeup, she is no high-maintenance prima donna. Wing is kind, considerate, and generous. She rarely let me pay for anything during my three-day visit to her family's home in the nearby town of Qiong Lai, she kept me plied with delicious food prepared in the family kitchen, and she made sure my teacup never ran dry!

Nor is Wing a stranger to hardship, having spent a summer working for McDonalds at 50 cents an hour and still suffering from sleep-deprivation from the stifling dorm conditions endured by students here at CDUT.

My delight in being with such a drop-dead-gorgeous miracle vies with disbelief!

The beauty of Imogen, meanwhile, who did take up my suggestion of a Shakespearean name, is more understated and incrementally revealed, as when she wore a dress to a friend's wedding and I noticed the champagne shape of her calves. Now in her first year at CDUT, Imogen came to me as a dance partner. She is also a kindred spirit in loving poetry.

What to do with "this great sea of joys rushing upon me"?[21]

Thirty-Six

I had taken hold of Imogen's hand once before, when we walked together one evening in downtown Chengdu. And so I felt emboldened now to take her hand again, this time across the armrests in my teacher's apartment.

Our heads inclined, I felt the warmth radiating from her face, our cheeks touched, until finally our lips came together and drank deep.

"You give me much water," she said. I chuckled. She meant I was always giving her cups of tea, but of course I enjoyed the double-meaning.

She asked me to explain. I told her that would be another time.

We placed a pillow on the adjoining armrests and our heads on the pillow.

Thirty-Seven

The first thing I noticed about Jenny is her sensational body — phenomenal in tight jeans. And she has just about the nicest bottom on campus. A few weeks into my informal Tango classes, which I began giving here earlier in the semester, she came to me with her phone number and said she wanted to show me Indian dancing.

A few weeks later, after she reminded me of her offer, I met up with her, whereupon she came to my apartment, turned on the tape player, and began a series of breathtaking gyrations.

Those tight jeans again, framing a supple waist that playfully winked at me as she raised her arms. A breast-jostling shimmy. Then her back turned to brandish posterior perfection.

So the Peacock Dance *does* have a rival after all, and this a private viewing!

On the way over, Jenny asked me what type of woman I like, and did I believe in love at first sight? Life just got a little more complicated!

Thirty-Eight

I sometimes jokingly think of them as "The Great Unwashed", having on many mornings walked behind some students badly in need of a shower. When bathing requires the inconvenience of a 15-minute walk from the dormitory — towel and change of clothes in hand — and a 15-minute walk back, they can be forgiven some neglect in the personal-hygiene department.

But must they snot on the floor during class? Given the sickening levels of pollution on campus, of course one needs frequent pulmonary discharges, but this practice of hocking loudly and projecting the resultant effluent on to the ground indoors as if it were a trophy for public viewing, is quite beyond the spittoon!

Not that it's much better outside. There are hedges, gutters, garbage cans, even tissues, that could serve as receptacles for bodily drainage. But no! The snot and saliva are deposited wherever the offender happens to be, from mouth and nose alike, leaving the rest of us to dance around the output, hoping not to get it on our shoes!

The last time a student did this in class, I stopped mid-sentence, whereupon the boy sheepishly apologized, then atoned for his indiscretion by spreading the phlegm around the floor with his foot!

This phenomenon, along with other classroom pastimes such as nose-picking and nail-clipping, call for tuition in manners as much as language!

Thirty-Nine

My earliest memories of vegetables from my days as an English schoolboy are the soggy, bland, boiled-to-death servings that collapsed exhausted and denutrified on to my plate, accompanied by the admonition that eating them was "good for you." And my subsequent experiences with this food group only confirmed the unfavorable early impressions.

But how things have changed since I came to China! The surroundings of Chengdu are blessed with an abundance, variety, and richness of vegetables and fruit that must be seen, and tasted, to be believed. Almost every week, it seems, some new offering from the neighboring countryside shows up in the market near the campus back gate — often something I have never seen before.

I enjoy my forays to this part of the campus, provided I keep my distance from the construction trucks churning up and depositing choking clouds of dust. The area presents a symphony of appetizing smells at mealtimes — punctuated by the occasional discord of "stinky tofu" — as local vendors prepare steamed buns, noodles, egg fritters, hotpot, fried potatoes, porridge, and raisin cakes. At night, the scene is a shimmering mirage of light and steam, reflected in the swollen waters of the river.

I have a favorite dish now — yú xiāng qié bǐng — battered eggplant slices stuffed with meat and served in a delicious sauce. I am also very partial to kǔguā hōng dàn, a kind of fried omelet with "bitter melon", and tǔdòu ní, meaning mashed potatoes, literally "potato mud".

My consumption of vegetables — prepared here with such creativity, flavor, and flare — must have multiplied tenfold since coming to China. I dare to think I'm even having a healthy diet!

Forty

In equal scale weighing delight and dole.

William Shakespeare, *Hamlet*

Pinky, Wingspan, Yankee, Cool George, Comfort, Exile, Medal, Cup, Wonder, Vapor, Yeti, and Bird. These are not the names of racehorses, sailing ships, or even pets, but what Chinese students have chosen as their English names! Not that I suggested any of these, of course, having provided them with a long list of choices from Shakespeare, mythology, and poetry.

As this academic year draws to a close, it's time to take stock, even to marvel at my survival! Many foreign teachers here didn't make it to the end. The premature departures of Megan, Stanley, Willem, Don, Ian, and Mary — together representing about one-third of the foreign contingent — speak volumes about the teaching environment here — misguided and mismanaged, condemning and corrupt.

But I made it to the end, I weathered the storms, and let none despise me.[22] I learned to be indifferent to the indifference, and to understand, as expressed by the apostle Paul, that "I remain free."[23]

Do the authorities try to confine me, my methods, or my subject matter? I remain free. Do they try to dilute my standards, destroy what I create, or call good "evil?" I remain free! Do they offer unsolicited advice or tell me how to feel? Yet do I remain free!

And I close out this year with many encouraging messages from students. Here are some:

> "Thank you very much for your patient instruction and all your classes about Shakespeare, which led me into a literary world full of inspiration and stimulated my desire to create a beautiful imaginary world for myself. There is still a long way for me to go to the palace of literature, but I will follow it with determination.

> "At last, I have nothing to do say but thank you. To me, it's a great honour to be your student."

> "Do you know that we, the students in my class, really 'esteem you?' They like the way you teach and it really made them happy. They would always remember the 'heartbeat in the English language,' the dance, and the music. I hope that I'll have the chance to learn your dance one day. It's so beautiful."

> "I want to thank you because you teach me so many things of the foreign culture and poetry. I am very lucky to have you to be my friend."

And then there's this one, bitter-sweet, from a former student at the broadcast college:

> "Yesterday, we watched the movie Shakespeare in Love. When I listened to their words, I thought they speak English like you, very beautiful British English. It reminds me of you. You act in the class,

recite the poetry. After we watch the movie, other classmates all have the same feeling. We miss you..."

I had planned to show them *Shakespeare in Love* myself, and with the proper preparation — giving them my own notes on the movie and testing them to make sure they'd studied them fully beforehand.

Of course, the Chinese teacher now in charge of their class didn't bother with any of that troublesome preparation, just screened the movie out of the blue.

What have I discovered? That I am a gifted teacher, that I can inform, educate, and entertain, and even enjoy myself in the process! And I have put together a powerful array of teaching materials from my own research. All things considered, I want to continue this adventure in China.

Laments From Leshan

One

Racing downstream in the Dadu River was a kind of double baptism for me, not just into the waters of Leshan, a city about two hours south of Chengdu, but also into the local community. As they sat in their innumerable tea houses lining the riverbank, they were thoroughly entertained to see a foreigner (or "lǎowài") among the droves of Chinese people floating downriver on a summer evening.

Our journey ended near the foot of the ancient and colossal Buddha for which Leshan is famous. Carved into the side of a towering cliff more than a thousand years ago, and suffused with the characteristic red glow of the local rock formations and soil, this statue in turn lies in the heart of a chain of hills that resembles a reclining person and is known as 'The Sleeping Buddha'.

Even more thrilling are the rides on the Number 2 bus, aptly numbered for the diarrheal speed with which it hurtles towards the campus front gate, "like a fart in a hurricane," to quote famed British racing driver Graham Hill as he described his first illegal experiments with nitroglycerine in the petrol tank.

Rolling and bouncing down the winding road like a demented monster pursued by a legion of fiends, the Number 2 blares its high-pitched and ear-piercing horn at every person, vehicle, bird, bush, or stone in its path, assisted by conductors reaching through the window and pounding the sides of the bus to warn tricycle-riders to get out of the way. Then, at each stop, passengers are pulled on board by any article of clothing these conductors can grab. The reason for such haste, I gather, is that bus drivers here in Leshan are financially penalized if they get one minute behind schedule!

When I tell my Chinese friends I swam in the Dadu River, they worry about the danger, but it's a picnic compared with the local bus ride!

Two

There was a maddening quality in this seeming resolution of the foe to give him no rest.

Stephen Crane, The Red Badge of Courage

Someone has discharged a lungful of phlegm on to the bare concrete steps leading up to my campus flat, with typical disregard for others. On each landing floor, in this ugliest of buildings, lies a great quantities of boxes, timber, and building materials that no-one ever bothered to move. On the landing nearest me, a pile of cement dust has taken up permanent residence.

And squalor prevails outside the building too. The ubiquitous cement dust, churned up into toxic clouds by every passing truck, bus, and taxi, coats the main campus road.

Beyond a brick wall marking the campus boundary lies a once-pristine haven of trees, dense with lush green foliage, a natural oxygen tank from which I hoped to breathe deeply, but over that wall is a large and growing pile of garbage tossed there by people too lazy to walk a couple of minutes to the designated trash area. And the trees themselves are often obscured by the smoke of bonfires.

My lungs were again assailed by one of these fires as I was swimming in the campus pool one morning, where the water is thick with flakes of human skin, and the sides slippery with algae and slime.

But, worst of all is the noise. My neighbors bang and slam doors and windows at all hours of the day and night, making the whole building shudder with the reverberations. I can not get to sleep until the last person has gone to bed, and must wake with the first person to get up. Throughout the daytimes, campus radio blasts soppy Chinese pop songs through ancient, crackling speakers built for much more modest volumes.

I feel tired, listless, depleted — a symptom of the sleep deprivation that has plagued me ever since I came to China about a year ago. And the scheduled classes, far exceeding in number the workload I was promised when I signed the contract, have not even started yet! No stopping to smell the jasmine for me!

The foreign-affairs administrator insists I am "too picky" with my requirements for a quiet place to sleep, that my problem is psychological, that I should accept the situation because the Chinese people don't have a problem with it.

That's not what I've heard. Students regularly tell me they feel "cheated" by the conditions here, and the younger Chinese teachers tell me they too are very uncomfortable in their surroundings and want to leave! But they are contractually bound to serve out five years on pain of a financial penalty equivalent to two years' salary!

Students have also told me of at least three foreign teachers who threw in the towel in previous semesters because they couldn't stand the conditions here.

The college has also reneged on its earlier promise to help me find a place to rent off-campus if the accommodation proved unsuitable. Not only are they refusing to help me now but, citing "security concerns," are barring me from living off-campus at all! A third promise was that the foreign-affairs office would replace my paper and printer cartridges, but now that I have run out, they say I am printing too much! Bricks without straw again!

Three

The college has just issued a decree banning teachers and students, on pain of dismissal, from patronizing any farmer-run restaurant on campus — this in a bid to expel the entire agrarian community living here, so that they can sell the land to developers.

The alternatives are not appetizing. Our class ran late today because the college failed to provide DVD facilities I had booked well in advance. When I finally sorted it out, and we finished watching our movie, all the food in the campus cafeterias, bland as it is, had run out. And we were forced to walk past the delicious smells coming from the farmer-run establishments, their doors open for business that will never come.

Now, I would be the first to welcome tidier conditions on campus, an end to the choking bonfires, the careless garbage disposal, the clamor of roosters, and especially the stinky manure pit near my lodgings. But does the solution have to be this draconian, depriving students of decent meals and entire families of their livelihoods? Is there no middle ground here that can preserve the best of what the local community provides while cleaning up the rest?

It seems the farmers are poised to take direct action. I wish them well.

Four

The murmur of a carpeted world is replaced by the clanging reverberations of steel doors and bare corridors.

Breyten Breytenback, speech given in June 2000

I can quite understand why the sleep deprivation practiced by U.S. jailers and interrogators around the world and by the KGB before them, is regarded as torture. It strips a person of autonomy and ultimately of hope, even paving the way to desperation and insanity.

Finally, the college has responded to my complaints, months into an exhausting teaching schedule ground out between restless, tormented nights trying to snatch moments of sleep between the bangings and slammings of inconsiderate Chinese neighbors. Then stepping out each morning past the fresh cigarette butts and phlegm to drag my weary body to class and, as D.H. Lawrence put it, smolder in "a heap of ashes of weariness."[24]

The college's answer? To move me across campus into a tiny concrete block with no hot water, no shower, no heating, no air-conditioning, no curtains, no furniture, no phone, no computer. No nothing, except for a bed so infested with mold that black patches of it stain the mattress surface, and smelling so bad that I could not sleep through a single night for the stink.

Same goes for the bedclothes, which I will have to replace at my own expense, if I can find the time.

Moreover, the floors and stairwells are coated with cement dust in this newly constructed building, and I will have to scrub the place down myself. Sure, China is a poor country, but poverty is not the problem. It is a fundamental disregard for health and human need.

I have, from first to last, been lied to, cheated, and deceived. Yet the foreign-affairs office insists I will have to pay a breach fee if I leave. To Hell with them!

Five

My first encounter with direct action in China. Yesterday, there were at least two altercations between farmers, starved by the college's embargo on their restaurant businesses, and teachers charged with enforcing the ban on students wishing to patronize them. The day before, farmers had blocked the road through campus, effectively closing a bus route.

I understand their anger. Some of the families have lived here for generations. Their tilled fields and harvests served as camouflage from U.S. satellites in the days when this site was a nuclear-research facility known as "585". But now that a campus is in place, the farmers have apparently outlived their usefulness.

Meanwhile, there is nowhere to eat. The only sanctioned place serving food now is the college-run cafeteria, which does not accept cash but requires use of a card that I have not been issued with, despite being promised one weeks ago. This means I have to take a bus (if it is running) to the town for meals.

Many of the students think the farmers have gotten a raw deal at the hands of this college, and a group of them got a letter of protest published in the local newspaper.

I support their efforts. Does that make me a Communist?

Six

In opposition to empathy, the corporatist mode of being instructs us that human life, like material objects, exists merely to be used, used-up, then discarded.
Phil Rockstroh, *countercurrents.org*, Nov. 23, 2006

How's this for innovative education? Take university students out of the classroom for the last six months of their three-year course, send them to a distant city, and put them to scrubbing floors, washing dishes, cleaning toilets, and serving food in a dingy hotel from early morning to late at night. At the same time, make a nice little sum by pocketing the proceeds from their labor. And if they dare to resist, tell them they will not be allowed to graduate!

Sound far-fetched? Well, that is exactly what is happening to my third-year English-major students, who are all heading off to Shanghai next week. They are not happy about it, of course, but told me in class today, "We can't do anything. This is what our leaders tell us to do!"

I keep hearing that things are improving in China, and had assumed this policy was some left-over relic from the Maoist era. Not so. It began this year!

They call it "work experience". But there's a better word for it: slavery!

Though I am grateful for the prospect of a reduced workload after they leave, I am dismayed by this latest example of brazen corruption in China's education system. My students also tell me they will sit a raft of final exams this week, but the teachers have already furnished them with the answers! And those that still manage to fail can buy the teachers off with "an expensive gift".

In this Dantesque descent through China's education system, each level is serving up fresh horrors!

Seven

Having just started talking to two lovely girls from the nearby teachers college one evening in Leshan, I was not in a hurry to turn my attentions to an elderly man who approached us on the sidewalk.

But I am very glad I did. Xièhòudé is one of Leshan's famous artists, a divinely gifted man, and now a dear friend. It was he who presided over my baptism in the Dadu River.

An exemplar in black-ink portraiture, combining images of swirling feminine beauty mingled with Chinese lettering, he is one of several internationally renowned painters Leshan has produced. Recently, Xiehoude took me to a nearby exhibition, where I was honored to rub shoulders with a distinguished assembly of local artists.

My companion for the day was a first-year student named Emma, who recently struck me into silent awe with the gift of a captivating still-life she had painted. I am blessed.

Eight

*Like a coating of glaze over earthenware
are fervent lips with an evil heart.*

*A malicious man disguises himself with his lips,
but in his heart he harbors deceit.*

*Though his speech is charming, do not believe him,
for seven abominations fill his heart.*

Proverbs 26:23-25

The most dangerous villains, as Shakespeare observes, are those with "a smiling cheek." In a simile I share with my students, he likens them to "a goodly apple, rotten at the heart."[25]

For the foreign-affairs administrator at this college, one Neo Li, feigned friendship is the favored strategy, first in recruiting me, but then in enlisting his mistress, another teacher at the college, as his spy!

I now realize her assignment was to befriend me and glean, largely through dinner conversations, my hopes and intentions regarding a hasty departure from this institution of iniquity. At the same time, she was a conduit of threats, disguised as friendly warnings, that the college would pursue me if I relocated to a teaching position elsewhere, and get my visa revoked.

I learned some of this intelligence from an English woman who briefly taught at this college last year. She describes it as "the most corrupt place I have ever been" and her stint here as "the worst experience of my life," a sentiment I readily echo. This place is killing me slowly, and I know not how many years have been etched into my face by its nightly regimen of violent sleep deprivation.

Meanwhile, Li is the only other person with keys to my lodgings, and I recently discovered, despite his pledge never to enter without talking to me first, that he had sneaked in here the other day while I was teaching class.

Scripture counsels me to be "wise as a serpent."[26] But I am in my enemy's land now, he has vast experience in working this turf, he knows the layout, knows the personalities involved, knows whose palms to grease, knows how to work the levers of power and, of course, the local language. Still, his powers of deceit and subtle brutality have earned my stunned admiration, even as his target!

Sharp his serpent's tooth, subtle his serpent tongue, his lies and threats skillfully concealed beneath a veneer of plausible humility, obsequious civility — a Chinese Iago or Uriah Heep, O'Brien from Orwell's *1984*, or Roger Chillingworth of *The Scarlet Letter*. He is all these rolled into one. Devilishly clever, not just here on campus, but in the way he treats his wife and seven-year-old son, whom he visits on alternating weekends in Chengdu while running his mistress in Leshan.

I have met many villains in my time — backstabbers, cowards, con-artists, schemers — and I considered myself adept in smelling the rot and discerning counterfeit from true. But I must admit in this case I was completely taken in, duped, spoofed, and suckered. Chewed, swallowed, and digested.[27]

So, with the Psalmist, I cry out, in the desperate, lonely hours of the night: "The cords of death entangle me; the torrents of destruction overwhelm me; the cords of the grave coil around me!"

Then may the Lord reach down from on high, take me out of these deep waters, and bring me to a spacious place.[28] Then may I see my enemy bound and gagged, his malicious tongue muted once and for all!

Nine

To "shanghai" means to "force or trick someone into doing something, or going somewhere." It takes on a literal meaning for my third-year students, now languishing in that city on the far side of the country for college-mandated "work experience".

One of them, Bryant, showed up unexpectedly at English Corner last Sunday, having fled back west across China. He tells me his fellow students are getting up at 4am every day, going by bus to their jobs, working for 12 hours, and finally returning to overcrowded dormitories with 12 to a room.

"I have been here one month, but it feels like a year," another student tells me in an email. She describes a tearful existence sweeping floors, cleaning toilets, or serving food. "Every day, we lack sleep," she continues. I can relate!

For Bryant, the bitter ashes of humiliation, too. When he arrived in Shanghai, they told him, "Your shoes are dusty from walking from Sichuan!" — meaning people from this province are considered too poor or too backward to take other transport. And things only went downhill from there, as the wages he earned waiting tables at Shanghai's Ramada Hotel were parceled out between his teachers and an agency!

Meanwhile, I'm hoping to make my own escape from Leshan. By bringing to this campus a well-connected friend from Chengdu, who has influence in the Communist Party and with the university that presides over this college, I have been able to secure a release letter, and the written promise I will be paid all monies owed.

Perhaps the hardest aspect of my departure will be to leave behind the kind and generous friends I have made among the students. One of them emailed me the other day: "I will miss you very much, because you are the best foreign teacher I have ever seen."

Ten

With film crew, journalists, and entourage in tow, I had all the trappings of celebrity as I viewed an exhibition of two local artists. Following me from painting to painting, they were eager to know what I thought of their work, hanging on every word as if the pronouncement of some oracle.

It didn't seem to matter whether I had any experience or qualification to comment. But I must have managed to make some intelligent noises, because we then all whisked off to a lunch of endless toasting, followed by the familiar Sichuan scene of supping tea around the mahjong table.

Again, I am amazed at the breadth and depth of artistic talent concentrated in this locale of Sichuan Province, and again I am overwhelmed by the warmth and generosity of the local people and students here.

My artist friend, Xiehoude, was in rare form, rattling off poems in Russian and Chinese, while my lovely student friend, Emma, was politely resisting the attentions of a local official. This fellow speaks not a word of English, but he later took great pride in leading me round town by the arm, showing off the "laowai" to his associates. He treated me to some desserts from the local bakeries, but thoroughly embarrassed me by not paying for them, while refusing to let me do so!

I have met many wonderful people through my connection with Xiehoude. Another friend of his took me to see Leshan's Great Buddha last weekend, where I thrilled to catch a glimpse of a rare and beautiful kingfisher bird as it scoped the waters near the Buddha's feet, as well as some other brightly plumaged species I could not identify. Before that, I was delightfully deluged by a crowd of teenagers on tour with their nearby school, who wanted to take pictures with me as if I were a film star!

Against this backdrop, the college administration where I am teaching stands like a desert in an oasis, but because there are no mid-year teaching jobs on offer in this area now, I must leave to take up my next assignment in a university near Beijing.

Still, the joys of Sichuan Province will stay in my heart forever.

Eleven

William is the kind of student every teacher hopes for — dedicated, diligent, disciplined, honest. For my birthday, he presented me with a verse written by the renowned Tang Dynasty bard of Sichuan, Lǐ Bái (c. 701-762 A.D.)

He not only meticulously rendered the work in four different styles of exquisite calligraphy — "regular script", "seal script", "official script", and "running script" — but translated the poetry into English.

> *I'm on board, we're about to sail,*
> *While on the shore they stamp and sing.*
> *The Peach Blossom Pool is a thousand feet deep,*
> *Yet not so deep, Wang Lung, as your love for me.*

Li Bai is called "Poet Immortal" by the Chinese. And I can testify, more than a thousand years after he wrote them, and even in translation, that lines of his have moved me to tears.

William is a leading student of his class, and recently won a coveted scholarship from the university. I am glad of this, for when I last met him near the campus, he was shivering with cold because he could not afford a decent coat.

Yet he did not win the first prize, which includes free tuition for a year. That went to another student who had cheated in his scholarship exam and who comes from a wealthy family closely connected with the head teacher.

I frequently hear accounts like this, confirming cheating and nepotism are rife in determining who gets rewarded in China.

But there is no doubt whom Eternity shall remember!

Twelve

It was a tearful farewell with Imogen, who began as my Tango partner in Chengdu but who has also been my girlfriend for the past several months. She has stood by me through my many recent trials, and brought cheer to my heart with several weekend visits to Leshan.

We just got back from a glorious trip to Lijiang in Yunnan Province. I could not have wished for a more joyous and caring companion, who thrilled at each new sight and experience, especially during a daytrip to the Leaping Tiger Gorge. As we neared its rushing waters, the rocks on the far cliff shimmered silver in reflected sunlight, singing of Heaven just around the next corner.

On our last day in Lijiang, I bought her a gorgeous outfit that somehow both encapsulates the local folk costume and serves as glorious attire for Tango dancing. She never looked sexier, yet it is her spirit that shines most beautiful of all. On our final afternoon, spent on a grassy hill overlooking the town, she shimmered before me in a dance of joy.

Now I am going to Changping, near Beijing, and she will be completing her undergraduate course over the next two years in Chengdu. Am I descended from Cain that I must wander this earth while it yields no reward to my labors?[29] Yet I treasure in my heart these precious memories.

Chidings From Changping

One

Nature was not so far removed, or hard to get at, as in these days.

Charles Dickens, *Barnaby Rudge*

My suspicions were first aroused when the parking attendant, after some minutes of conversation with our driver, handed him a wad of receipts. "Ah, that way goes the game!"[30] I thought, as we left Beijing airport and headed towards Geely University.

And when I arrived, having been assured by Geely's foreign-affairs representative that there would be "plenty of fresh air" here, was I shocked to see that this campus, like the one I had left behind in Chengdu, was also overlooked by the belching stacks of a power station? Or was I shocked that I should find it shocking to be fed lies again?

Worse yet, there is another smaller power plant burning coal right next to the apartment complex, its thick yellow-gray clouds swathing the area night and day!

The campus is pervaded by a permanent, dusty, toxic stink. The air is drenched with chemicals, my sinuses sting, my eyes water, my throat is parched, my skin begrimed with dust and soot. But this is not about poverty, it's about choices — about how people choose to live and build, or choose for others to live. Quality of life is disregarded in this equation.

And the campus itself is more desolate than any I have seen. Not a flower or plant in sight. No birds but scavenging magpies, whose nests dot the barren trees like dirty thumbprints. Threadbare verges along the street. Ramshackle slums of concrete and brick lining the entrance.

What's wrong with these people?!

Two

To perform a miracle is one thing, but to perform one where there is no faith, is beyond impossible![31] I met today with three boys who want private coaching for crucial exams this summer. Failure in those exams would mean staying behind in China when their classmates go off to England for two years of study.

It was an act of sheer desperation on their part. Short on effort but long on funds from rich parents, like many of the pupils at this private college, they can barely speak a few words of English, despite several years of classes. A more fluent student, whom they had brought along as interpreter, told me their lack of proficiency reflects lives spent playing computer games and basketball when they should have been studying.

Will they behave any differently now? I asked. Oh yes, they said. They would work hard now. Then the boy across from me snotted on to the restaurant floor and joined his friend to fetch some beers to the table.

I declined the gig.

Three

Well, if things don't work out with the girls, there's always the thrill of getting frisked at the local disco in Changping, where four policemen formed a human gauntlet on the way to the dance floor.

I don't know whether it's curiosity about the dimensions of a foreigner, or overzealousness in the performance of duty, but I was patted down with a thoroughness that might be described as "patting up" if it had gone on much longer. Still, stifling my laughter, I managed to make it onto the dance floor without international incident!

At the outset, there were far more policemen — helmeted and wielding truncheons — than punters, although none of the guests showed the slightest inclination towards violence. And if they had, I doubt the pudgy-faced youths assigned to protect the clientele could have done much about it!

At one point, the dance floor was cleared to make way for a chubby host singing countless karaoke tunes between swigs of beer, followed by a very tedious and drawn out kind of Bingo game.

Still, it was a good night out, and the company sublime.

Four

Absenteeism runs high at the Euro-American (Ōuměi) College at Geely. I'm now in my third week of teaching, and some students are just showing up for the first time. Others are there in body, having being roused from slumber by college monitors, but their spirits remain in bed.

Many, boys especially, have been up all night playing computer games — a growing affliction in China. Indifferent from the start, their heads are lying on the desks when I walk in and do not even stir to find out if the lesson is worth being awake for!

Sometimes I grind to a halt, stunned by the sheer stupidity of my students, by their inability even to answer the simplest question, though expressed in every variant known to man, and broken into the most elementary forms of language, or to recall what I had shared with them but two days ago.

These are the students whose parents have deep pockets but, in a system where private universities are allowed only to recruit from the dregs of failure in national entrance exams, academic wealth runs inversely to financial wealth. My former students in Sichuan, many the sons and daughters of farmers, were on the whole brighter, more enthusiastic, and more conscientious.

Beijing may have its intellectual bright spots, but Geely University is certainly not one of them!

Five

My teaching materials have just been rejected. The college is refusing to photocopy them because they don't see the connection to the students' final exams. My work, the fruit of countless hours of study and devotion, is dismissed at one stroke in a veto process involving an administrator, a Chinese teacher, the vice dean of the college, and anyone else who feels entitled to sit in judgment! This, in spite of assurances before I came here, repeated upon arrival, that I could teach whatever I wanted!

The college is also complaining that I am not using their official textbook. Of course not! It's rambling, incoherent, and full of spelling and grammatical errors. But again, I was told before I came here, that I wouldn't *have* to use it!

Nor did anyone mention exams these students will sit in a few months. It's called a "hospital pass" in the game of rugby — someone passes the ball to you just as you're about to get nailed! These students have for so long been so woefully ill-prepared, ill-disciplined, ill-motivated, and ill-taught, that success is beyond impossible!

Many should have been kicked out long ago. It would do them and their parents a favor. But that would mean less income for the college. So the fraudulent exchange of papers — banknotes from students' parents, meaningless certificates in return — is continued.

Those who do make it through the exams are admitted to a two-year study program in Grimsby, England. I asked my students the other day how many they expect to pass. "Half," they answered, followed by the reassurance that most would go to England anyway "because our college has a good relationship with the college in England." O good! Let them become someone else's problem!

Six

That's odd. I just had an email bounce back with the message "rejected for Sector 5 policy reasons." Is there surveillance going on behind the scenes?

One of the foreign teachers has warned me that some students here are used as spies, while administrators and local teachers are encouraged to pry information from foreigners and report it to government officials, in return for promotion and rewards.

That such a covert operation exists is not hard to believe, given the levels of *overt* surveillance already conducted! The college employs a carping cadre of clipboard-wielding busybody bureaucrats who throng the corridors by day and peer into the classroom every few minutes, justifying their parasitic and superfluous existence by reporting on the activities of others!

I must also sign in at the front desk every morning and afternoon, get a guard to open a padlocked gate to enter or leave the college, wear an ID tag at all times, fill out an assessment form at the end of every class, get an assessment form filled out by an anonymous student and a weekly assessment commenting on my work, and be visited without prior notice by administrators inarticulate in the English language to watch and judge my performance!

All this, they say, is "university regulations," though I know foreign teachers in other Geely colleges are not subject to the same routine indignities.

And now I am told there are "complaint letters" about me from unspecified students about unspecified matters which "may be forwarded to the principal." I gather it takes less effort to complain about a teacher who refuses to give out a free pass than it does to follow standards that might promote learning!

I have some of the laziest, dumbest students who ever wasted oxygen in a classroom. They should have been sent home months ago to reflect on their life choices and face the music from fee-paying parents. Most don't have a clue even about basic scholarly disciplines, such as keeping the teaching materials I gave them last time, let alone filing them or bringing them to the next class! Many don't even bring a pen! The idea of completing homework is beyond foreign to most of them, and only a handful bother bringing a dictionary to class, meaning I have to spoon-feed these intellectual infants with every word predigested for them in Chinese!

Fuck you, Geely University! Fuck your oversight. And fuck "Sector 5"!

Seven

It all depends on your point of view, I suppose. The word "country" to me evokes images of rolling fields, sturdy trees offering their shade on lush green pastures, babbling brooks, cozy cottages, and birdsong.

But here, "country" means something quite different: stinking streams and filth-strewn drains, rapescapes punctuated with brick shacks and roadside rubble, clouds of dust everywhere, barely a blade of grass in sight, and all set in a dismal wash of concrete grey. Nature is smothered, stifled, crushed, obliterated, defiled. It is impossible to be indifferent to the ugliness. It steals over the heart like an infernal shadow, eclipsing all hope.

Outside the campus, the walk to a nearby row of restaurants requires passing a ditch full of discarded filth. The stench is unbearable. I was shocked a few months ago to see a woman toss a bag of trash into Leshan's Minjiang River, but here every body of water is a communal garbage dump, every stream an ulcerated, running sore whose natural mechanisms of repair are overwhelmed by the perpetual reinfection of relentless effluence.

And then there are the sandstorms, sending flocks of students scurrying for shelter, hands over their faces, eyes half closed against the swirling fury of desert winds scouring the campus, and unmitigated because of deforestation. Sand in the eyes, sand in the teeth, sand in pockets, and even coating every surface inside.

Apparently, all the foreign teachers heard the same recruitment pitch: that the campus is "in the country" and far from the pollution of Beijing. In reality, our remoteness from the capital only means it's enormously time-consuming to get there.

So we end up with neither country nor city benefits here, unless of course you count the rat running through Dining Hall Number Two the other day in broad daylight!

Eight

Louis, another foreign teacher here, was given a raise for his part-time work at Renmin University. And Renmin is not an educational backwater like Geely, but one of China's top teaching establishments. But after this noble academy changed Louis' teaching hours without prior notice to times that clashed with his prior commitments elsewhere, they reneged on the promise.

Meanwhile, neither of us has received overtime pay our Geely contracts specify. Nor does any foreign teacher have the health coverage we were promised.

Administrators in China lie; it's really that simple — habitually, casually, without compunction. They nickel-and-dime and cheat and do not honor their commitments, either verbal or written.

I often hear the defense that China is a "developing country" to justify these kinds of behaviors, and it rings more and more hollow each time. This has nothing to do with insufficiency of financial or material resources. No, the impoverishment is spiritual, cultural, environmental.

And educational. The other day in class, when I asked students for words and phrases about myth and legend, they turned it into a paean to Chairman Mao, describing him as "great," "responsible," "gifted," and "strong."

So I enquired further as to the source of this revisionist hagiography. "Do you all think this way?" "Of course!" they chorused back. "How do you know?"

"We read it in the book our teachers gave us." "Who wrote the book?" Silence.

I too have begun a part-time job at Renmin. I hope they pay me the princely sum of 100 RMB per class that I was promised. The main reason I took the work is to use the university's swimming pool in the afternoons before class, preferring it to the dry hole in the ground that must account for Geely's boast on its website that it has two pools on campus!

And so the pattern continues!

Nine

Here is a note I prepared for my students. After a Chinese friend translated it, I distributed the bilingual copies among them.

Beijing Geely University is not noted for its academic prowess, but even within this campus, the students of the Euro-American College have a reputation for very poor standards.

I ask myself why? These are the students who have the most advantages, whose parents can afford to put them in an expensive program and send them overseas. Why then, do so many have no willingness to learn, let alone the enthusiasm and hunger for knowledge shown by my previous students in Leshan? Why do the sons and daughters of poor farmers, truck drivers, or construction workers in the economically depressed province of Sichuan outperform their wealthy cousins in Beijing?

I suppose it's because of a phenomenon we in the West call "failing upwards" or "flying too high on borrowed wings". Or we might call it "The George W. Bush Syndrome" — that a person who has failed in everything he has done, be it education, military service, or business ventures, someone without the slightest motivation or intellectual energy, somehow ends up in a position of power simply because of family connections and wealth. It's a kind of money-

solves-everything existence. And look at the catastrophic results for humanity!

Is that the way the world works? Is that the kind of world you want to live in? Do you want to live in a system where people fail upward and where money solves everything?

We have another saying in the West: "Life is too short..." Is life so long that you can afford to waste four years of it in an academic institution where you study nothing, learn nothing, and gain nothing? Does your life have so little value that you would throw it away?

And do you take the easy way out and blame others for your underachievement? Do you blame your teachers? Do you scorn the journey of discovery they have set out for you? If so, your teachers deserve better. The college has recruited talented and dedicated people to help you. I know this, because I am one of them!

And have you heard the saying: "Without a dream the people perish"?[32] What is your dream? Have you chosen life?[33] Or have you chosen the spiritual death of ignorance?

What will lift you and motivate you to study? Fear of your parents' anger? Never. Fear will never sustain you. So don't study for your parents, do it for you, do it because you want your life to mean something!

Believe me, there are many harder things in life than studying for a degree. There are much higher mountains to climb, more dangerous paths to tread. I know something of this, having experienced exile, homelessness, terrorism, devastation of my health, and bankruptcy. Compared to the trials of life, education is a picnic. But if you will not even rise to this easy task of studying now, how will you ever survive, let alone prosper, when faced with the true troubles of life?

Are you building your house on rock, so that it can withstand the future storms — for they will come — or are you building on sand, so that you will be swept away at the first little trouble?[34] If you have built on sand — and many of you have — it is time to abandon your shoddy work and the pattern of your past and start the true labor of digging in rock.

The time is short. Act now, before it is too late!

I gather my observations have raised a storm of protest, though one of my more motivated students privately said to me, "I totally agree with you." Her opinion, of course, must "o'erweigh a whole theatre of others."[35]

Ten

Two buses barreling down toward us, side-by-side, devouring both sides of the road. A head-on collision averted only because our taxi driver — himself unlicensed and uninsured — swerved into a neighboring field (or, more accurately, a patch of mud).

Overtaking round blind corners, weaving across highways jockeying for the best position, trucks overfilled with cargoes improperly secured and swaying dangerously along treacherous lanes. These are the prevailing practices on Chinese roads.

One of the foreign teachers here, enquiring about obtaining a Chinese driving license, was offered answers to the written test in advance if he paid a bribe of 1,000 RMB.

So here's another of China's paradoxes, that a country rigid with censorship and repression, bent on controlling the lives and activities of citizens and employees alike, lets anarchy reign on its highways and byways!

Eleven

When I first met Imogen, I did not imagine she would become my girlfriend; and when she became my girlfriend, I had no idea our relationship would take us on vacation together and continue after my departure to distant Beijing while she remained in Sichuan. And when I came to Beijing, I never imagined I would be steadfast to her when I had opportunities to be with several gorgeous girls here.

But Imogen's place in my heart has grown steadily since I first met her as a potential dance partner over a year ago. Besides, I am about to leave the educational arena, with its many romantic opportunities, and head to China Radio International as a newscaster.

Our geographical separation is a challenge, however, as are my meager financial resources. Meanwhile, her parents don't want her to be with a foreigner!

How much time have I wasted fretting about all this?

Briefings From Beijing

One

It's a curious coincidence. China Radio International (CRI) refuses to call Taiwan's leader "President", insisting that the island is part of China, and nor will I refer to George W. Bush as "President" after he stole two U.S. elections! Instead, in my newscasts I am calling him "U.S. leader, George W. Bush".

But while I was recording, I could see in peripheral vision the desk editor in frenzied conversation with the head of Overseas Broadcasting, whom she had just called in.

I have just finished my first week at state-media organization CRI. My role is to select, update, edit, and read on air an hourly news segment, five minutes long, plus two half-hour in-depth news shows per day.

Scripts for the latter, being prepared by non-native English speakers, require a lot of editing to make them readable and engaging. And often, because my colleagues are unnecessarily late in getting them to me, I have to improvise as I am recording!

The workload is brutal, inducing a barrage of fatigue-induced headaches for most of my first week. I expect it will get easier, but the labor is far beyond my early days as a correspondent at Reuters in London and New York.

The sources from which I draw are confined to CRI's own editing system or website, and the Xinhua news agency. Still, there are some interesting things to glean, such as data showing 30% of Chinese households have experienced domestic abuse, a report that traffic cops in Guangzhou have an average life expectancy of 45 years because of pollution, and the imprisonment of peaceful protestors by Kenyan police.

The prisoners were released the day after my broadcast. I'd like to think I had something to do with it!

Two

They are splendid specimens — strong, slender physiques, chiseled features, belts, buckles, leather shoes all shining, spick and span, polished, buffed, and pressed. They are the sentinels at CRI's gates, granting admittance with waist-high salutes, and their numbers have doubled in the lead-up to the 2008 Olympics.

But whatever shows of bravado adorn CRI's exterior, on the inside dwells a culture of timidity. Of course, I expected reporting on China itself to be highly circumscribed, but I was not prepared for the level of paranoia in reporting on other countries.

For example, in a script I prepared on an International Red Cross summit to discuss the treatment of civilians by military forces, I was not allowed to quote a Red-Cross report saying U.S. treatment of prisoners was "tantamount to torture."

"The U.S. embassy might be listening and might get offended," I was told.

Anyway, I have been taken off newscasting for failing to confer on Mr. Bush the title of "President", but can perhaps now carve out an alternative role recording audio books.

Three

Though I have left Chinese academia for the time-being, I still get treated to gossipy anecdotes from student friends.

Apparently, discipline has been stepped up at Chengdu University of Technology (CDUT), my first employer in China, as it prepares for official inspections. Every morning, new messages are broadcast over the loudspeaker system calling for discipline and even reminding students to make their beds! And those who show up at the school gate after 11pm curfew get written up on a public notice board the next day. One girl was publicly denounced for "indecency" after she was seen kissing a boy on campus.

The effect of such puritanism, of course, is to drive liaisons off-campus, where there's a roaring trade in one-night room rentals.

But the anecdotes can also take a macabre twist. I learn of murders, suicides, and rapes at various campuses, which the authorities are quick to cover up but are well known on the student grapevine. A boy jumped to his death from a campus building; another drowned himself in Leshan; a girl was raped near the gate of Beijing Geely; and a student murdered a teacher at CDUT.

Perhaps I got out just in time!

Four

More brick walls as I attempt to put together features reports at CRI. Among the material vetoed: a story about a character in a novel being gay, a documentary film criticizing Hollywood stereotyping, and comment from an interviewee citing pollution as a suspected factor in leukemia.

So what are we left with? Fluff about dancing geese in Guangzhou and Flamenco performances at Beijing's Poly Theatre!

Horseshit! Timid, tepid, insipid, flag-waving, propaganda-peddling horseshit!

Five

Huaguo Mountain, in eastern China's Jiangsu Province, is more than a thousand miles from Sichuan's Emei Mountain, which I visited about two years ago. But its monkeys have the same mindset as their distant cousins, as I discovered when one suddenly leapt onto my shoulders from a nearby tree.

These primates are primarily preoccupied with primal urges — food and sex — and tourists are no more than a meal ticket, a moving buffet on legs. But don't say you weren't warned! A notice at the entrance helpfully points out: "The careful counter-attack guarded against is invaded [sic]."

To my relief, the creature wearied of me and jumped off, and I was left unscathed. But poor Konstantin, who works for CRI's Russian-language service, was not so lucky. His enthusiastic picture-taking of a baby put its mother on the defensive, whereupon she delivered a savage bite between Konstantin's shoulder blades, landing him in hospital for a rabies injection!

Still, Konstantin remains better suited to the nightly regimens of this official CRI trip. After meetings with local bureaucrats keen to get photo-ops with the laowais, we are seated at the top table for dinner to join a chain-smoking, wine-guzzling Chinese brotherhood, who loudly belch, spit on to their plates, and bully the waitresses catering to their gastronomic whims and insulting behavior.

Konstantin manages to keep up with their relentless toasts, while my polite refusals to imbibe the headache-in-a-bottle Chinese red wine, much less the lethal baijiu rocket fuel, are met with bafflement and incredulity. Given the exhausting schedule of the days, I am not keen to add sickness to fatigue.

And this legend-rich part of China affords so much to take in. Notwithstanding the misbehavior of his kin, one monkey at Huaguo enjoys huge fame. He is Sun Wu Kong, the Monkey King himself, protagonist of the epic Chinese novel, *Journey to the West*. According to the story, he was born from a rock at Huaguo, where he dared to enter the Water Curtain Cave, a mountain tunnel veiled behind a waterfall, which we also visited.

The elevation of Huaguo is only 600 meters, but what it lacks in height, it more than makes up for in tall stories. One Buddhist temple, for instance, showcases a rock fragment inscribed with an intricately carved Buddha — made not by human hand, they say, but by miraculous combustion!

In November 2006, the Buddhist master Neng Kuan died at the age of 94 after several days of fasting and reciting scriptures. With her last breath, the weather suddenly turned to rain, and it continued raining for seven days. But at the end of that time, at the very hour set for her cremation, the rain suddenly stopped, and a ray of light pierced the dark clouds and alighted on the pyre. By the end of the ceremony, a glorious rainbow arched over the scene.

But the miracle didn't stop there: among the ashes were several crystalline fragments, of which the largest bears the unmistakable image of a perfectly etched Buddha in seated repose. All this without human intervention!

Then there's the claim that the people of both Japan and Korea are descended from a single Chinese ancestor. According to locals, one Xú Fú left the area in search of immortality during the Qin Dynasty and went on to father these two nations.

They cite as evidence several visits to Lianyungang, the main city of this region, by former Japanese Prime Minister, Tsutomu Hata,[36] seeking his ancestral heritage.

Another intriguing tale is that of the poet Zu, a kind of Chinese Cyrano, reputed to be so ugly that no woman would consider him as a husband. So he enlisted a handsome friend to pose as him, reciting his verses to a beautiful woman. But when his new bride discovered the ruse, she promptly deserted him. After that, Zu retreated to the life of a hermit at Huaguo.

And there are living legends too, such as a pair of Gingko trees, said to be more than 900 years old, that overlook a nearby courtyard. One afternoon, after I dozed off in a tea pavilion next to them, lulled by the sound of rain splashing on the flagstones outside, I awoke to find the ground carpeted with their yellow fruit, followed by the quick appearance of local women gathering it up by the bucketload.

The next "mountain" we visited was Dayishan, even shorter at 227 meters but, in the words of the official brochure, an "airy-fairy fairyland" with "queer rocks" and "grotesque elements". Its informal name is

"Shuìměirén", meaning "Sleeping Beauty", because its outline resembles a woman reclining on her side.

A number of important ancient artifacts have been discovered here in recent decades, some dating back more than 6,000 years, including the earliest known sarcophagus in China. There are also cliff paintings from the Yuan Dynasty.

Dayishan also has its share of myth, including the *Legend of Baige Gully*, which tells of a young fisherman who loved seagulls. But to his horror, his father suggested they eat the birds. In a dream, the spirits of the gulls came to him as beautiful maidens. They told him they would solve his dilemma by flying away, but he would find them again at Baige. Eventually, he was reunited with them there and became immortal too.

The next destination in this pinball tour of four "mountains" in two days was the waterfall-adorned Yuwan, beneath which a family of dragons is said to reside. I guess every country has its variant of the Loch Ness monster, but China has conjured more creatures of the imagination than most.

Having said that, artistic expression is still proscribed. At Confucius Mountain, we saw a Ming Dynasty poem carved into the rockface but partly erased. Apparently the author, Lin Ting Yu, a former civil servant who had versified his disgust with the government that dismissed him, smoothed over two lines of invective for fear of the consequences if he left them. As one of my Chinese colleagues observed, "even back then, we were afraid to say something against the government."

The party line is also very much in evidence on the island of Liandao, which is connected to the mainland by a causeway. There, a sculpture depicts six smiling, waving figures, including former Chinese leader Deng Xiaoping, all looking eastward with covetous gaze towards Taiwan in hopes of a "One China". But ironically, the six cheerful characters also overlook a demolished fishing village, cleared to make way for a tourist hotel.

Underlining the orthodoxy throughout were the local officials, all in short-sleeved white shirts, all wearing black trousers clinging to middle-age paunches with the help of black belts and silver buckles. Off we all went, our minibus surrounded by their cavalcade of shiny black European limos, from one wearying meeting to the next, where yet more officials would answer yet more pre-scripted questions with pre-scripted answers, which we journalists should faithfully record.

But the first prize for political correctness goes to "Kàng Rì" — literally "Anti-Japanese" — a scenic area devoted to China's "proletarian revolutionaries"[37] and "patriotic education".

After all the officialdom, meeting Zhang Ji Zhong, director of a new *Journey to the West* TV series, was a welcome change of pace. I got the impression, though, during our Q&A, that this latest remake will gloss over the story's mystery and metaphor in favor of martial arts and special effects.

Our final afternoon afforded welcome respite at the hot springs of Donghai, where the mineral-rich spring water comes from the ground at a searing 83 degrees Celsius, after which it is piped through various reservoirs to cool down.

One hot-water site excluded from our itinerary, however, was the nearby Tianwan nuclear power plant, now operating two of four planned reactors. Still, we did get to see some of the thousand or more Russian technicians and experts collaborating on the project as we boarded the plane back to Beijing. What was it that caused those deep grooves in their faces — cigarettes, vodka, or radiation?

Still, I get the impression environmental protection is taken more seriously here than in other parts of China. It seems half the rooftops, even of the poorest dwellings, have at least one solar panel. And the administration of Donghai reports it has closed down polluting factories that flouted environmental standards. Certainly, my lungs felt clearer during our few days in the area after the consumptive air of Beijing.

Finally, one last shaggy-dog story: among the many industries now residing in the Lianyungang area is the Wang Lao Wu dog-meat company. Just to be clear: the meat is not *for* dogs but *from* dogs, including "dog meat jelly", "dog stomach", and "dog tongue"! These, the company claims, have "magic effects on health." Well, they would say that, wouldn't they?

I would like to return to this area one day, though without the accompanying officials and official expectations. For here, fact blends with fiction and folklore with fantasy. As a friend once said to me, "Never let the truth interfere with a good story!"

Six

We were discussing the environment, at my part-time teaching job with a private company in Beijing, when one of the students offered a remark of unusual insight. "Spiritual pollution," he said, is a problem in China.

It's certainly the case at CRI, not just with the censorship, dogma, and dumbing down that infect broadcasting, but also in the employment practices. Along with late salary payments and threats to withhold salary, my contract is being repeatedly revised to encompass a growing workload.

I thought my job was to record audio books, now they've added copy editing and hosting a live show. They said at first I needed to produce four audio-book episodes a week, now it's five. Moreover, I should be able to achieve this without reading the books in advance!

And when I protest, it's the same old refrain Chinese employers always use: the Chinese workers get it worse than you, so why are you complaining? As if two wrongs make a right. I will need a lot of detox after CRI!

Seven

"I will never complain about China again!" Or so I told myself as I left the Armed Forces Hospital in the west of Beijing. I had gone there for help with a skin cyst under my chin. I'd had an operation in the U.S. before, but it only partially and temporarily dealt with the problem. This time, I would be navigating an unfamiliar medical system in an unfamiliar language in an unfamiliar country.

The first pleasant surprise was a greeting from three tall and glamorous girls at the hospital entrance, all dressed like flight attendants in matching uniforms, followed by yet more beauties operating the lifts. But these were all trained nurses, I later found out.

The first doctor was a kind and gentle spirit. My friend, who came with me to translate, told me his referral note to a specialist said I should be charged a minimal fee. And that specialist himself was another kind soul who could speak English. He and his assistants took me to the operating room, swathed me in pristine sheets to keep me warm, and proceeded with the utmost care and attention. All in all, it was like gliding through a sea of gentleness.

After a couple more trips through the hospital's halls of glamour, I had my stitches taken out and gave the surgeon a heartfelt thankyou card.

I have also got together with a couple of the nurses. Meanwhile, the long-distance relationship with Imogen came to an inevitable but peaceful conclusion, and she now has another boyfriend in Chengdu.

Eight

I thought it was one of those routine inspections to check my registration when the police showed up at my door last night. But when one of them said they were taking me to the police station and advised me to "cooperate," an icy dread began to creep into my heart.

I told them I had to go back to work. "No," they said. "We have already talked to your boss. We need you to come with us." He showed me the photograph of one of my work colleagues, a student from Singapore, who had begun a six-month internship at CRI a few weeks ago.

Immediately, the whole nightmarish picture began to come into focus. This girl had come to my apartment two nights before, distraught that her boyfriend was on his way from Singapore following her confession she had slept with another man. Me!

Her boyfriend, she explained, believed she was a "victim" and wanted to get the Chinese police involved. She hadn't told him — crucially, as it turned out — about the *second* night she spent at my place!

As I crammed into the back seat of the police car next to two fat cops, I started to contemplate my future. I was in trouble, I seemed to be a suspect, and my employer was involved. What would happen? Would I lose my job? Would I be kicked out of the country?

After walking with my minders into the police station, I was escorted to a room where yet more officers were waiting, all speaking Chinese, no-one speaking to me. What was going on?

My anxiety grew. After several minutes, I could wait no longer. "What's this about?" I said. Two of the cops spoke a little English. One of them showed me the picture of the girl again.

"Do you know her?"

"Yes. She's one of my work colleagues."

"She's charged you with rape."

Oh my God!

They wanted me to make a statement.

"I should have a lawyer here," I said.

More unintelligible conversation between the bluecoats in Chinese.

"Under Chinese law, you cannot have a lawyer now," they said. "Someone from your office is coming."

I pondered the possible outcomes. People convicted of rape in China get the death penalty, don't they?

I did my best to stay calm, but I must have been the picture of terror when a Chinese colleague from CRI arrived.

Again, the police insisted they question me without a lawyer. Again, I resisted.

Back and forth, back and forth.

Then I was relieved to hear that the girl had withdrawn the rape accusation, saying our sex was consensual. It was only her boyfriend who was insisting they press charges.

So if the accusation has been withdrawn, I said, why do I need to make a statement?

"We need to hear your side of the story."

"Will what I say be recorded?"

"It will be written down."

"What if she reasserts the original charge? Then what I say could be used against me?"

More back and forth, back and forth.

I finally agreed to make a statement after another CRI manager called and said I wouldn't lose my job if the sex was consensual.

I proposed to write a statement in English, which my CRI colleague would then translate.

They agreed to this, whereupon I described how the girl and another intern stayed at my apartment that night, how she had decamped from the sofa to my bed, how we had consensual sex, making every effort to be quiet so as not to disturb the other girl in the spare bedroom, how I made breakfast for them both the next day.

I went on to describe the girl's second visit four days later when she again came to my bed, again had breakfast with me the following morning, and stayed on to watch DVDs with me and then have lunch. Then I described her third visit, this time to relate her anxieties about her boyfriend's imminent arrival in Beijing.

By this time, the air was fogged with hours of cigarette smoke from the chain-smoking cops who thronged the office.

My words were then translated verbally to the uniformed entourage. They gathered round to look at the piece of paper, though written in a language they did not understand. What's the word for that? Prurient? Vicarious? A written translation was produced. Documents were photocopied, photocopies photocopied.

Then I was presented with a form to sign, saying I had been brought to the police station for questioning about a rape charge!

"But you told me the rape charge was withdrawn," I said via the translator. "I made my statement on that understanding."

More back and forth, more back and forth. Angry words in Chinese directed at the translator. "You must do this!" he conveyed. "This is Chinese procedure; this is Chinese law."

But why would I sign something saying I had been charged with rape, when they had told me I hadn't been charged?

Yet more back and forth, back and forth. More angry words, more cigarettes, eyes watering by now, numb worry and fatigue.

In the end, the translator signed the form himself with a statement saying that I had refused to.

In total, the ordeal lasted more than three hours.

In the subsequent days, I have been spooked every time a police car shows up in the car park of my apartment complex, in case they're coming for me! Now I know what it is to fear "the knock on the door in the middle of the night!"

Nine

Young men will do't, if they come to't.
By cock they are to blame.

William Shakespeare, *Hamlet*, IV.v

"I'd love to sleep by myself just for once." So spoke my dear friend Dwain, yoga partner, former teaching colleague, and part-time filmmaker. He made this comment when visiting me and was responding with apparent envy to my big, empty, unshared bed.

A tall, strapping black man from the U.S., 25 years old, with chiseled features and powerful eyes, Dwain is clearly a major draw for the local lasses. When we were both working at Geely University, he was living with one student, enjoying occasional dalliances with another, and having an affair with the university administrator who recruited him!

But his stock of condoms couldn't meet the demand. Late one night, he showed up at my campus apartment asking if I had any to spare. Even so, within a few days he was touring local stores seeking a fresh supply, and I enjoyed the spectacle as the amused staff gathered round him in a cluster of curiosity while, despite language difficulties, he doggedly pressed his case.

But things came to a head, so to speak, when the live-in girlfriend, also a karate expert, slammed the other student in the neck. I saw the bruises that proved it! Dwain also had a scare when the first missed a period, though it later turned out to be a false alarm.

Now, Dwain has another teaching position at a private company in Beijing, where he is continuing to collect student phone numbers. And, though his first girlfriend from Geely is still living with him, and his schedule much busier, he is still managing to run one bit on the side along with, in his own words, a "cougar".

He is envious of me?! The randy dog! I should be envious of him!

Ten

Foreigners' salary payments at CRI are a week late this month, perpetuating our anxiety about whether the company will keep its part of the bargain. We hear that the foreign-affairs office is again in dispute with the financial department, while managers of the English Service are contributing contradictory statements of their own. All are quick to pass the blame, but that doesn't help us!

I quote from a brave email openly written to management by my Australian colleague, Paris:

> *In what has become a monthly ritual, we foreign staff were paid late, and once again, no-one paid us the courtesy of explaining where OUR MONEY was...*
>
> *If there are continuing problems within the CRI fiefdoms, why must our pay be caught in the middle of it?*
>
> *Why does no one in the CRI English Service office bother to explain...?*

Meanwhile, I am not allowed to go on vacation because, eight months into the job, they are still revising my contract. Having downgraded my salary in one revision, they quietly removed two vacation days for Christmas in the next and turned a once mandatory travel allowance into a conditional one based on employee "performance". And, in the process, the size of this document has more than doubled to reflect "new laws and regulations."

Unionize! I hear you say. Good idea! My complaints are, after all, standard fare among foreign employees here. Well, Mao be praised, we *do* have a union, though there has never been a single meeting. And our shop steward? The same department manager who has been downgrading my salary while adding to the workload and responsibilities.

Run that by me again? We don't get to elect our own representatives? No. CRI selects the representatives who will negotiate with themselves about how to treat us!

Meanwhile, the Chinese government is touting how it wants to attract foreigners to work in China! Well they won't get many at that speed!

Eleven

I have ridden subways in the cities of four continents, but none compares to the overcrowding in Beijing.

Even at my stop near the western terminus of the One line, inbound trains are already standing-room only. Then, with each successive stop, the remaining air gaps are filled with body odor, alcohol fumes, and garlic-laden breath, all marinated in the blood-corrupting vapors of solvents used in the perpetual construction at or near stops.

A simple increase in train frequency would alleviate the overcrowding, but that would require commonsense or sustained political pressure from a populace dulled by "two thousand years of kowtowing," to quote Lin Yutang's 1935 commentary, *My Country and My People*.

Twelve

"Sign the contract, or we will cancel your visa!" That's the latest threat from CRI management who in the most recent revision of this pernicious document have shaved off vacation days, halved the permitted number of sick days, and revoked the promise of a round-trip air ticket home.

Meanwhile, they have introduced new clauses enhancing management power, such as permission to withhold salary payments for up to a month if an employee flouts unspecified "rules and regulations."

Oh, but I must give credit where credit is due: management has offered me an alternative freelance arrangement if I will take half the amount of money for the same amount of work!

This in the context of a work burden so intense that it has begun to shrink one of my eyes! In a condition known as ocular myasthenia gravis — with the fitting acronym of OMG — my left eyelid has begun drooping, presenting to my horrified gaze in the mirror a spectacle of disfigurement.

Unlike audio-book narrators in the West, I must not only make my recordings single-handedly but edit them and configure them into episodes! Moreover, as I am narrating translated Chinese literature, the process requires fixing textual errors and figuring out Chinese pronunciations.

The strain of continually staring from book to computer screen and back again has taken this disfiguring toll, but in response to a doctor's note saying I should take two weeks' rest, the deputy director of CRI's English service, one Li Peichun, scoffed before claiming, "the doctor is irresponsible." He has even refused to provide a simple book stand in the recording studio, let alone a computer-screen filter, to ease the strain on my eyes.

It's curious that he shares the same family name, Li, as my former nemesis in Leshan. I am inclined to decry that entire clan!

He has also complained I haven't recorded enough audio-book episodes, even though CRI has made no effort to broadcast any of the hundred or so I have already produced after enormous investments of my energy, time, and love.

They're not even available by internet, even though I have designed a website to host them, complete with my deeply researched background information on the books, the authors, and their times. I have even included my own renditions of poetry by China's Tang Dynasty "Poet Immortal", Li Bai, the subject of a brilliant novel by Simon Elegant entitled *A Floating Life*.

Meanwhile, CRI is continuing to use my voice for soundbites, narrations, and promos for their other radio shows and pet projects without a penny of extra compensation.

With only three months left on my contract, I signed it, and am saving what's left of my vacation time so I can leave as soon as possible.

Thirteen

This time, it's the turn of my friend and colleague Paris to run afoul of management.

The other day, he came to me asking what I thought of the headlines he selected for his newscast the previous day. I told him they struck me as very "Asia-centric." His lead story, and the longest, was about China's three-day mourning period for victims of the Sichuan earthquake. The following two headlines were about a humanitarian crisis in 'Myanmar'. Only one headline — the last of seven — referred to something outside Asia.

What I didn't know, when Paris showed me this, was that Mr. Li had complained Paris' script choices were not Asian *enough*, that he should have said more about China's mourning for the Sichuan earthquake. In short, "the broadcast was intolerable," and Paris was "immediately suspended" from newscasting.

The pharisees are sharpening their knives again, straining gnats of perceived omission while swallowing camels of their own silence[38] about the world's genocides, rapes, and lies. Furthermore, news scripts are signed off by a senior Chinese person at CRI before broadcast anyway. They get a free pass on this, but Paris has now been fired!

I was one of four foreign employees Paris came to for our perspectives on his news selections. He did so at management's suggestion. Having reported back the largely supportive findings of his colleagues, management now wants to question us!

Bloody Hell! It's such a Keystone-Cops operation here. Laughable, if it wasn't so vicious!

Fourteen

The feelings of Chinese people after the Sichuan earthquake are following a similar pattern to those of Americans following 9/11. Shock and disbelief at first, followed by an outpouring of aid and sympathy. Then citizens start to ask how the tragedy could have been avoided or at least mitigated and wake up to the government's complacency beforehand and incompetence after. Then, the government responds with a cover-up and repeated calls for patriotic compliance. In the end, deep distrust rubs salt into the wound of trauma, loss, and grief.

One of my former Leshan students, Evelina, whose family's home near Mianyang was obliterated, tells me the government is deliberately understating the number of dead, while many "volunteers" have been helping themselves to loot.

Some of my U.S. friends have contributed money to Evelina's family, while the foreigner community in Beijing is organizing fundraisers. As for what's happening on the ground, I'm getting a more accurate picture from my friends than anything state media is serving up!

Fifteen

A couple held a bowl between them and, with chopsticks poised, raced each other to the center along their respective strands of noodles. Their daughter looked on, laughing. And I looked on at them all, rejoicing in this snapshot of happy family life. The couple saw me and, with an exchange of smiles, we all rejoiced together.

These are among the treasured moments of living in China, interacting with the people met every day, enjoying their warmth, their greetings, their help, the innumerable expressions of welcome.

But most of all, I have enjoyed the children, their mesmerized curiosity as they gaze up at me, sometimes uttering a "hello" if they can get past their shyness, or sometimes, with their parents' encouragement, calling me "ShuShu" ("Uncle").

So now I am faced with yet another strange paradox about China — that this nation of kind hearts can harbor such fiends in the workplace!

Being so reticent in expressing anger, the Chinese people have fostered a culture of impunity among those in charge. And the predations of the Maoist era are but one branch of this poison tree rooted deep in Chinese history. As Lin Yutang points out in *My Country and My People*, published in 1935, the Chinese put up with "more tyranny, anarchy, and misrule than any Western people will ever put up with."

I have so often been driven to exasperation, exhaustion, and near despair in almost every job I have done here, but there is no recourse to be had, no appeal to reason, justice, fair play, or third-party intervention. Instead, I am ever met with, at best, savage indifference.

And Chinese administrators are such an inscrutable breed, drawing perhaps on a tradition of deception as celebrated in *The Romance of the Three Kingdoms* or on Daoist principles about feigning ignorance. Certainly, they adhere to Confucian ideas about trusting one's "gentlemen" rulers who must never be touched by law or reproach. I am out of my depth here, too many moves behind in this infernal chess game of plot and subterfuge, feint and threat.

A friend asked me the other day, "What do you think of the Chinese people?" I answered, "They make very good friends and great hosts; I have always felt very welcome as their guest. But I wouldn't want to work for them!"

Sixteen

Narrating *A Floating Life*, the brilliant novel by Simon Elegant, was by far the most challenging project I took on at CRI. The longest of the seven audio books I recorded, with many long and complex sentences, it requires two distinct narrator voices, in addition to a large cast of characters.

The main voice is that of the legendary Chinese poet of the Tang Dynasty, Li Bai, who lived in the 8th Century A.D., as he dictates his life-story to a scribe. Meanwhile, the omniscient narrator describes the poet's process into exile on a barge.

Moreover, I needed to serialize the book into 25-minute episodes. This involved another set of choices about where to begin and end each one, either to be a self-contained story or to create suspense for the next, while moving the overall narrative along. I even recorded and edited an interview with the author himself, now living in Beijing. Enormously complex and time-consuming, but I am very happy with the result, both artistically and technically.

And how strongly I identify with the main character! Just as Li Bai is feted at a court banquet, stunning the guests with poetry improvised and recited "as it flows from his brush," so did I win acclaim in a recent presentation to CRI's English Service about my new and groundbreaking series, *Alight on Literature*.

I entertained the assembly with a wide range of characters and accents, demonstrated how to make readings dramatic and lively, explained the process of serialization, and shared some of the painstaking research I had prepared.

But just as Li Bai's long treatise setting out a wise course to the emperor, is ignored in *A Floating Life*, so my creation — to which I gave birth; devoted my gifts and labor day and night; protected, nurtured, and championed through every stage of its perilous journey — has never aired! Nor has the station posted on its website the system of pages I designed for the series, where I set out the fruits of thorough research about the books, their backgrounds, their themes, and their authors.

Li Bai was never comfortable at court in Chang'an (modern day Xi'an), China's capital at the time. Bold and outspoken in his verse, visionary in his understanding, impatient with the follies of officialdom, he inevitably became a target of palace intrigue.

Here at CRI, it is not in my nature to compromise on the quality of my work, even in the face of management's spiteful and punitive obsession with quantity — quantity for quantity's sake that resulted in a vast treasury of material never broadcast. Nor could management's ignorance or indifference infect my love. Still I was devoted to the project heart and soul, even if the whole thing would turn out to be an exercise in futility.

"Wasted! Wasted!" as the poet himself cries out in the book. "A waste of breath and spirit!"

What motivates CRI's murder? What malice stirs in the heart of that little emperor Li Peichun to hide this light from the world? Fear? Insecurity? Jealousy? Maybe all of these.

I pray for my episodes: "O Lord, liberate my children. Let my people go![39] Declare over them: 'Do not touch my anointed ones. Do my prophets no harm!'"[40]

Now I join the long roster of foreign employees spun through CRI's revolving door — another commoditized, used up, and exhausted human being.

Seventeen

Though I am a citizen of both Britain and the U.S., it is Team GB I most root for when it comes to sporting events. And my loyalties were richly rewarded in these 2008 Olympics in Beijing, where "we" came an amazing fourth in the overall medal standings.[41]

The Chinese audience around me at the Water Cube swimming venue were amazed by my exuberance as Rebecca Adlington clawed her way past U.S. swimmer Katie Hoff, in the final stages of the 400 meters freestyle, to win Gold. Adlington would go on to win the 800 meters a few days later. That morning, I saw four World Records broken, with two additional Olympic Records! Glorious to witness.

Then, at subsequent evenings at the Bird's Nest athletics stadium, I saw another Brit, Christine Ohuruogu, win the 400 meters on the track and Germaine Mason take Silver in the men's high jump.

And all this enjoyed with beautiful girls beside me! Eva came with me to the swimming event, Anna to my first outing to the Bird's Nest, Stacy to the second, and WuQing to the third.

But at the Water Cube, another hot girl came into view on the other side of the stadium, seen with the aid of binoculars. I didn't know that I knew her until I spotted her father in the chair beside her. There he was: politician, baseball-club owner, and the reason I was removed from newscasting at CRI, one George W. Bush! And the girl I had noticed beside him was one Barbara Pierce Bush.

My only regret with these Olympics was not taking advantage of my apartment's proximity to the cycling venues in the far west of Beijing, where Britain would win 14 medals in all!

Eighteen

What a send-off! What a magical evening! I have just witnessed a spellbinding production of the "tribal rock musical" *Hair* at the outdoor Delacorte Theater in Central Park.

Musicals are not usually my thing, and I was disappointed I hadn't got back to New York in time for the prior production of *Hamlet* at the Delacorte. But I soon forgot about that as this cast of beautiful and extraordinarily gifted actors reprised the show first staged in 1967 by the legendary impresario, Joseph Papp. That was before he got the Delacorte built following a long and hard fought campaign. And, with Hamlet's "I have of late..." speech set to song in this musical, there was even compensation for missing the play!

The live musicians were phenomenal too, including my former saxophone teacher, Allen Won, playing an array of woodwinds. Even Nature collaborated, so that when the lyrics refer to the Moon in her "Seventh House," there she was, shining resplendent, stage left!

Looking back over my three-week stay in New York, all seemed divinely orchestrated. Beth's spare room in Park Slope happened to become free for a week on the very day of my arrival, then I spent a few days with Abraham in the same neighborhood, before staying with my dear friends and former Tango students, Neal and Philippe, on Roosevelt Island. And home-cooked meals from all! Furthermore, Philippe was on one of his rare second-shift weeks (as a translator at the U.N.), giving him time to drive me to the airport for my return flight to Beijing.

I learned through the experience, in testament perhaps to Jesus' "lilies-of-the-field" metaphor[42], that I need not worry about the "hows..." in all uncertainties I face.

It also struck me anew, as it did when I first came to New York back in 1991, what a magnificent cast of characters inhabit this vibrant city. I met up with Richie, the most loyal friend a person could ask for; with Yan, my ex, whose love of life is heartwarming; with Horst, a man for all seasons and a walking treasury of wit; and with Ariel, a noble outcast from New York's community of cut-throat lawyers.

And there was Peter, who has shown unparalleled courage in recovering from brain surgery and in whom burns a holy flame, defying convention and insisting on living life to the full; Abraham is a fellow refugee from Corporate America; Beth, a diligent seeker after Truth; and Yuwei a highly principled and forthright journalist.

These are my brothers and sisters. I am blessed to know them. And their names are written in the Book of Life.[43]

It was also an opportunity to enjoy again a few of my favorite New York things: the English restaurants *Tea & Sympathy* in Manhattan and *The Chip Shop* in Brooklyn, the Aussie establishment *Eight-Mile Creek*, *Mariebelle* hot chocolate on Broome Street, *Uncle Louie*'s peanut-butter-cookie-dough ice cream, the Brooklyn Botanical Gardens, Prospect Park and, of course, the belovèd Delacorte with its adjoining Shakespeare Garden in Central Park.

And there were blessings anew: visiting the little havens of rest created by Roosevelt Island residents in their community garden, and sailing on New Jersey's Tom's River!

It struck me, too, soon after I touched down in New York and was ambling down pathways dappled with sunlight in Prospect Park and listening to the birdsong, how denatured Beijing has become, with its population of four surviving bird species — sparrows, pigeons, magpies, and jays — and its highly concreted areas wishfully called "parks". Nature survives when people fight for it! But I don't see that spirit at work in China.

It was also refreshing to behold the many shades of female beauty in New York, to get a seat on most of my (off-peak) subway rides, to have passengers letting me off the train before they come in, and drivers stopping to let me cross the road in front of them.

Perhaps it was a blessing in disguise that I was more or less forced to revisit New York. In true Olympic spirit, the authorities in Beijing refused visa renewals to thousands of resident foreigners in the approach to the Games, requiring us to return to our home countries and reapply!

Worse, Beijing's Public Security Bureau told me in August I would have to leave China *before* the Olympics began, even though I had already bought tickets! It was only after a protest and referral to another line that I was able to get a grudging and very expensive two-week visa extension! By contrast, the

Chinese Consulate in New York were much more user-friendly when I applied for my next visa there.

So I will now return as an unemployed foreigner to one of the most polluted cities on earth, concerned for my health, suffering from near-perpetual headaches, and financially depleted. As we sit on the tarmac at JFK, waiting for a much-delayed take-off, and the foul-breathed Chinese man next to me is absent-mindedly picking his nose and smearing his mucus on to the newspaper he is reading, I ask myself why?!

It can only be an act of faith. Lilies of the field. Lilies of the field!

Nineteen

As if to confirm Olympics window-dressing is over, all the flowers that graced the roadside outside my apartment have been removed, and in their place are empty plastic containers.

I had forgotten, during the recent Olympics prettification, just how revolting the air in Beijing can be. Now that it's back to business as usual, a constant milky film blankets the air outside, a lingering smell of dust and chemicals. Even inside my apartment, the smell of construction products seeps in, while floor drains in the shower area daily emanate a sewage stench like living in a permanent fart.

Meanwhile, the worst aspects of Olympics "security" measures have been retained, such as requiring everyone to put their bags through x-ray machines for every subway ride. Tedious and troublesome, especially when people try to cut in front, as is the prevailing custom here.

Twenty

"You're going to take off her clothes, and then she's going to take off yours."

Oh well. If I have to, I have to!

An agent submitted me for an evening party at the Hilton Hotel near Liangmaqiao as an Argentine-Tango performer, and I was to bring my own dance partner. But things turned out very different when I showed up.

For one thing, the organizers had chosen a partner *for* me, a stunning Chinese girl wearing a teeny-weeny miniskirt as part of her sexy police outfit. She was to be my partner in a kind of mimed sadomasochist dance-theatre piece involving whips, chains, and velvet-wrapped handcuffs, and culminating in a pose of passion and domination on the hotel bar!

I made a good go of it, though I'm glad none of my friends were there and that I was performing to mostly inebriated strangers I would never see again.

This is one of various jobs I have been doing in this new freelancing phase in China. Another was playing saxophone in a band organized by an Argentinean singer, even though I hadn't picked one up in more than a decade and was given a rather cheap instrument that wouldn't play the lowest notes, and accompanying songs I was hearing for the first time!

I have also done my first TV commercial, which meant putting on a chef's hat and pretending to enjoy the flavor of some very bland ice-cream. And I have just been cast in a production of Lyle Kessler's play,

Orphans, in the role of Harold. Meanwhile, I am attending an improvisation workshop, and there may even be some modeling in the offing.

What? Exotic dancing and modeling at the age of 45? Stranger things have happened, I suppose. And I am taking better care of myself with regular workouts, now that I am free of CRI's punishing schedules and demands. All this is interspersed with part-time teaching jobs, along with some editing work for Chinese students applying to U.S. universities.

Christmas Day was miserable, though. No-one showed up for my English class in the afternoon, but I had to stay there anyway, and though I did have full attendance for my evening class, the subway ride home was the saddest of my life.

New Year's Eve, however, was a joy, with friends visiting to play games, sing songs, drink wine, and watch episodes of Mr. Bean.

Money has been extremely tight. I was down to coins after shelling out more than 2,000 RMB to renew my visa for a lousy six months. That makes my fourth visa in less than a year!

Still, there is much to look forward to. This weekend, I am celebrating my birthday at the weekly ballroom-dance gathering at SinoChu wine bar. Next week, the Beijing Cheese Tasting Society meets. Every month or two, a member returns from a trip abroad with 10 kilos of artisanal cheese, and we get together for a tasting, complete with good-quality imported wine, a raffle, and a quiz.

I am also looking forward to the next 'Chocojing' event. The last one, at the Renaissance Hotel in Shuangjing, included dinner, mulled wine, and European chocolates. Finally, we got to dip a range of sweets and fruit in a chocolate fountain.

Even with all this going on, though, I am sometimes overwhelmed with loneliness and paralysis.

Twenty-One

"The company is filing for bankruptcy, and the accountant ran off with the passwords for all the bank accounts."

Well, at least that's an honest answer about why I haven't been paid for some teaching work. Thing is, I am already late with my rent! Meanwhile, another company has failed to pay me for a voiceover recording.

I have been living a freelance existence in Beijing now for about six months, and my financial situation is at best precarious. I could do without this latest setback!

Twenty-Two

I never imagined when I came to China that I would get the chance to reprise my former life as an actor. But I am back in the saddle now as Harold in the "gritty, realist" drama *Orphans*, to be staged at the Penghao Theatre. Harold is supposed to come from Chicago but we made him from London to accommodate my accent.

At the first rehearsal, I met my two fellow cast members — Nick Ma, playing the character of Treat; and Kris Chung, playing his younger brother, Phillip. Both are Chinese-Americans who grew up in the U.S. and great actors!

Kris was right into his part from the very first reading, including a hilarious impersonation of an urban black man, required by his part. Kris is an actor of Protean proportions, and equipped with a broad range of character voices. And Nick emerged with a menacing portrayal of the thuggish Treat.

Fuck! Can I keep up with these guys?

Twenty-Three

Orphans is a triumph, and press reviews of my performance as Harold — "brilliant", "charismatic and charming", "intense conviction", and the like — have been very encouraging.

My heart is overflowing with gratitude for this my first stage role in China, the latest in a series of new experiences: first saxophone performance in China, first booking to be a TV presenter, first television commercial, and my first photoshoot for a magazine!

I am feeling more optimistic these days!

Twenty-Four

Just one week to the opening of *A Midsummer Night's Dream*, where I will play Oberon in a bilingual production with Western and Chinese actors. It works beautifully to play opposite a Chinese-speaking Puck, as so much of the play's comedy hinges on misunderstandings between the two.

Both of my fellow *Orphans* actors are back for this too, with Kris directing the show as well as playing Bottom/ Pyramus, and Nick playing Francis Flute/ Thisbe. Kris is as fine an actor as any I've seen, and that includes productions of *Shakespeare in the Park* in New York City and the Royal Shakespeare Company! His antics for the death throes of Pyramus always have me weeping with laughter, no matter how many times I watch. In the words of another cast member, "It never gets old!"

And our *Orphans* producer, Anna Grace, is mounting this show too under the banner of Beijing International Theatre Experience — or "BITE". Highly energetic and resourceful, she is a veritable force of nature in the theatre world.

Back at CRI, meanwhile, I hear that Mr. Li Peichun greeted news of my revitalized acting career by blacking one of my eyes on a promotional poster pinned up by a former colleague. This destructive impulse mirrors the very real occlusion of my left eye brought on at CRI by the working conditions he imposed!

Meanwhile, the station continues to suppress the spoken and written treasuries I created there, but at last my voice is heard in Beijing!

Twenty-Five

The Central Academy of Fine Arts (CAFA). It's a high-sounding title, isn't it? Conjures the idea of lofty and inspiring values; lives lived in search of Truth and Beauty; spirits soaring to the heights of poetic imagination. The reality, though, when I came in as a substitute teacher, was rather different.

Of course I've dealt with students conducting cellphone conversations or texting during class. They usually respond with a sheepish acknowledgment of their disruptive behavior and stop, but this particular girl fumed with resentment.

Later, when I asked her to do a very simple acting exercise, she spent far more time arguing why she shouldn't do it than it would have taken just to get on with it. In the end, I asked her why she had invested all this time and money in the course when she didn't want to participate. This provoked her to greater anger and a complaint to the effect that I was saying she was "wasting her life." Well, I kinda *was*!

She proceeded to whisper in her neighbor's ear while refusing to participate in any way, then picked up her phone again, this time to video-record me! What was she doing? Collecting "evidence"?

Still, I am happy to report that, though she was the second-worst student I have ever encountered, she evoked nothing like the inner disturbance caused by the first-worst student all those years ago in Chengdu.

I must have come a long way since then!

Twenty-Six

"I'll never let you go!" So said a gorgeous student to me as I walked into the Fu bar last Sunday afternoon in Beijing.

She was rehearsing her character, Inez, from the play, *No Exit*. But as she was looking directly at me with those dark alluring eyes when she said it, the effect was, to say the least, arresting.

I had assigned her the task of developing four distinct characters for an acting workshop I am now conducting.

These days, I am rarely teaching English any more, as my life in China has gradually shifted into full-throttle immersion in the performing arts.

And I have upgraded my lifestyle too. I recently moved from the far reaches of western Beijing near CRI's headquarters, which entailed miserably overcrowded subway rides to get anywhere interesting, and am now living in a more tranquil area near Chaoyang Park.

Though the rent is more than double what I was paying before, the benefits more than compensate. I can get to my various freelance jobs with less stress and wasted time, and Western-style stores are a short rollerblade away. My social life has also taken a sharp upturn, hosting occasional gatherings in a fine apartment and dating three head-turning beauties. And I regularly swim at a 50-meter pool a short walk away.

My next stage performance, again produced by the indefatigable Anna Grace, will be a solo series at Penghao — comprising my one-man adaptation of *Wind in the Willows*, where I play 12 different characters, and two pieces by my favorite 20th-century poet, W.H. Auden, as Herod in *The Massacre of the Innocents*, and Prospero in *The Sea and The Mirror*.

If things go according to plan, I will also bring to Penghao a production of *Shakespeare Reveries*, an improvised drama using only Shakespeare's texts.

There's not much money in the theatre stuff of course, but through connections made there, I am now doing a lot of voice-recording, mostly educational material for English-language textbooks. Meanwhile, I have been in TV dramas, TV commercials, and even a film recently shot in Beijing by the U.S. SciFi Channel. I'm getting more work as an actor here in China than I ever did in New York!

Does this reflect my own development or reduced competition for the roles? Perhaps both. Anyway, I am living a much happier life now.

Twenty-Seven

God, what a clusterfuck!

Sitting in a car with darkened windows, I was driven to a film studio on a Beijing military base, having been instructed to put on a baseball cap and a hoody to conceal my Western features from guards posted at the gate.

The base houses China's military propaganda machine, where they churn out film epics and television series retelling the nation's glorious exploits of the 1930s and 1940s — first against Japanese invaders, then with Mao Zedong's defeat of his Kuomintang enemies in the civil war, followed by his triumphal investiture as Chairman of the People's Republic in 1949.

The first time I came to this base — under the same cloak-sans-dagger arrangement — was to dub another World-War-II film in which, because of poor sound recording, the original dialogue of its Western actors was almost inaudible. They had me dubbing an American general, having declined my suggestion it would make more sense for me to dub the British ambassador with whom he was conversing.

And I knew the guy playing the American too, Beijing-based Canadian actor Michael Gralapp. I asked the talent agent why he wasn't dubbing his own lines, but couldn't get a straight answer from her. I later learned from Michael, not best pleased by this turn of events, that they wouldn't pay him enough for the work. I wouldn't have agreed to the pay either for this long and complex project, but had been led to believe it would be a straightforward narration rather than dubbing.

But now, this second visit to the military base would take me down a whole new rabbit hole. First, I was preposterously garbed in Chinese military uniform, complete with dangling medals, and instructed to "say anything" to camera — I chose the nursery rhyme, *Hickory Dickory Dock*. I was there to sing the praises of some Chinese medical product or supplement called '007', which comes in a silver box adorned with the U.S. flag. The gibberish would then be dubbed over in Chinese for domestic consumption.

The director, a young woman, remained seated at a monitor in a dark corner at the far end of the studio, from where she issued conflicting instructions through an interpreter. And when all of this got confusing, she told me I was "wasting her time." Meanwhile, various intermediaries were turning, twisting, pushing, pulling, prodding, and poking me into desired position until I was seething with frustration. I finally returned the compliment: "You're wasting *my* time!" To which the reply came, "Just do what the director tell you [sic]."

And it wasn't just me getting pissed off. There was a general mood of resentment and frustration among the entire crew, and one of the Chinese actresses walked off the set in tears because the director was abusing her and subjecting her to endless identical takes.

The girl was obviously way out of her depth and totally inexperienced as a director. That might be OK in a talented person with good instincts. But she was neither. Meanwhile, during breaks, I was forbidden to step outside the fumy studio with its chemicals and cigarette smoke to enjoy the sunshine, lest I be apprehended by the guards. Even trips to the reeking toilets around the corner were by car to conceal my foreign appearance!

Finally, as we drove off the base at day's end, I suggested to the agent that the director must be sleeping with one of the generals to get this job. He guffawed and replied that she was far too ugly for that! True. A general's daughter, perhaps!

Twenty-Eight

How's this for exemplary English? "The economical prices of dishes are recommendable." Or "The traditional stores need to pursue after the Product Diversity if the want to survive [sic]." Or "Noise is disorderly for one's ear to bear."

These are among the sentences I am supposed to record for Chinese students trying to learn English by listening to CDs that accompany their English-language textbooks!

Here are some more: "appropriate frustration education is not bad"; "while on the train, we chatted, had jokes"; "the price of taking train is reasonable, but I can't bear the notorious condition"; and "What did the theft done to the girl's bike?"

These literary gems are the output of Chinese teachers who fancy themselves adept in English, and symptomatic of an education system replicating its own errors and far more interested in generating revenue than imparting academic excellence.

Of course, I alter the texts as I read them, as does my dear friend and main voice partner, Rebecca Parr, whom I affectionately call my "Voice Wife". My "Voice Mistress", Cath Marsden, also corrects as she goes along, but sometimes a publisher will come back and tell us to revert to the original errors because the book "has already been published."

Obviously, the publisher would be shown up by the discrepancy between a correct recording and an incorrect text. But I put my foot down when one studio instructed me to revert to "Her birthday falls *on* June," as opposed to the "*in* June" I had recorded.

A stand-off ensued, lasting more than an hour. Am I not in China as a champion of the English language and of academic standards? Should I read nonsense just so others can save face?!

They finally relented, though not without attempting a last-ditch trick: "Please record your corrected version *and* our original." Nice try! Of course, they would just erase my corrections! No way!

Meanwhile, I have approached several publishers with my own teaching materials built up over the years. In general, I get one of two responses: "All our books are written by Chinese authors, not foreigners"; or "Your materials are wonderful, but we need something more exam-oriented."

What can I say? This is *my* "frustration education", disorderly for *me* to bear!

Twenty-Nine

I gained more insight into China's film industry today, having been hired to teach several young Chinese actors preparing for *Deep Sleep No More*, yet another of these World-War-II movies that China turns out on an almost weekly basis.

In our first class, it was fun to lead the actors through warm-ups followed by spine alignments that unleash the full range and power of the voice, then to explore the physicality of characters. And I was looking forward to the second class today, in spite of the long journey to get there.

But when I arrived at the production office, a little room full of desks and filing cabinets and two uncaged budgerigars flitting overhead, I was told we would be having the class there, not in the same studio as before. Meanwhile, the office staff kept working on their computers.

The producer had also promised to provide me with yoga mats for the warm-ups this time. When I reminded them of this, they laid out one small blanket on the floor, and placed a bamboo mat on top.

"How many actors am I teaching today?" I asked.

"Five."

"How many mats do we have?"

"One."

"But I need six mats in total, one for each of the actors and one for myself."

"Why?"

"So we can do the warm-up. I explained all this to Mr. Jin on the phone."

"Can't you do one actor at a time?"

"Then the entire class would be a warm-up!"

I also explained that the actors would be emotionally vulnerable during the class and that we needed a space that allowed for a sense of trust and safety. A cramped and busy office, with clattering keyboards, people coming in and out, busy or idle conversation, and dive-bombing budgerigars, would hardly be conducive!

In the end, I came away with nothing but an unpaid apology. But the producer did offer me a consolation prize. I would be playing a role in the movie myself, he said, either as a Jewish merchant or a German captain.

He then directed me to a promotional photoshoot for the film. But when I arrived, the first person I saw was another foreigner clad as a Jewish merchant! I then recognized an Aussie guy I knew from a previous job and now dressed in Wehrmacht uniform.

"What role are you playing?" I asked.

"A German captain."

I see. Well, I have been well and truly duped today! As one of my British friends commented when I told her the day's events, "That's so Chinese!"

Thirty

Twitching muscles in my neck woke me this morning, the latest in a series of scary symptoms that have beset me in recent months. In May of this year, after a regular workout on my rowing machine, I noticed stiffness in my left thumb and looked down to see that the muscle at its base had all but disappeared!

Since then, things have become even worse. Both thumbs are now weak and stiff. Rapid atrophy in my arms has left skin hanging where muscle used to me, and my forearms, in particular, have withered like twigs. Meanwhile, numbness has spread all over my body, even to my face! I seem to be wasting away, deforming before my own eyes!

Suddenly, too, I have seen the flexibility of my spine, which I had maintained so diligently with yoga, diminish. I am going downhill fast, fearing the rapid decay of my body will culminate in a life not worth living. To someone who has lived life as an athlete, dancer, and actor, who doesn't smoke and rarely drinks, all this is beyond distressing.

Constricted nerve conductivity is at work, though we are at a loss to explain it. Tests so far rule out both motor-neuron disease and auto-immune disease, and scans of the neck portion of the spine show only very minor degeneration that the neurologist believes cannot be causing symptoms so severe. So we still don't really know the cause, and I am led to suspect all sorts of scary possibilities involving diseases I have never even heard of before!

I strongly suspect the heavy-metal toxicity that began with my proximity to 9/11 when I lived in New York City. Lead, in particular, is known to reduce nerve conductivity. Thallium is also implicated. But my Western-medicine doctor in Beijing tells me the Chinese government does not permit independent testing for such toxins. All tests must be submitted to a government-registered lab which, he tells me, has NEVER issued an abnormal result! Independent tests of air and water quality are also outlawed in China.

I shouldn't be surprised by this. In 2007, when I produced a report for China Radio International about a leukemia center for children in Chengdu, station management purged a comment by one of the volunteers that pollution might be a causal factor.

Not that you need investigative skills to know how bad the pollution is. In November every year, and until the middle of March the following year, China fires up its coal-burning power stations for heating, right in the middle of urban populations! Thus, chimneys dotted all over Beijing belch clouds of heavy-metal-laden smoke day and night. And though I recently read an article in Chinese media saying these facilities no longer operate within Beijing's Fourth Ring Road, I can see right now from my apartment window columns of smoke vomiting from chimneys between the Third and Fourth rings — in other words, inside the supposed exclusion zone!

For now, I am continuing with hospital visits to find out what I can, while pursuing traditional Chinese medicine (TCM) treatments involving bitter-tasting herbal concoctions and acupuncture.

Thirty-One

It's not the kind of medical facility we're used to in the West, but it does invoke a sense of the human family. At the TCM clinic I attend near Dongsishitiao, we, the ranks of stricken humanity, lie side by side on narrow cots, each in quiet repose and various states of undress, bearing the acupuncture needles or hot cups hastily applied by the harried and constantly interrupted doctor.

It's communal medicine in a tiny room, where sheets, needles, and glass cups are shared. Though the needles are put in a flame for sterilization between patients, I prefer to buy my own disposable ones at the entrance for the doctor to use. The patients here jockey for position too, reminding me of the pool at Bethesda, where the disabled man could not get to the healing waters in time.[44]

Still, there is a strong sense of community here, that we're all in this together. Prick any of us, and we bleed.[45] We learn about eachother's symptoms, and treatment strategies becomes a topic of group discussion.

I close my eyes and return to a deep contemplation of mortality.

Thirty-Two

I first met Cherry at a wine-tasting a year ago, a stunning silken-haired Chinese beauty, whose slender bottom I joyfully clasped in long bouts of thrilling love-making, pressing her alabaster skin hard against mine. God, how I loved the way she felt, her fragrance, her taste, her touch.

Divinity of Hell![46] For she who embraced me so ardently, whether in Chaoyang Park in Beijing, or the coastal town of Xiamen in her home province of Fujian, or even in a Paris hotel room and on a riverboat on the Seine, she who dissolved in my arms and nestled to my poetry, was ever a pillar of ice in-between, barely communicating for weeks at a time, even months!

Between our passionate but infrequent encounters, she remained distant and aloof, as tantalizingly out of reach as Stella in Charles Dickens' *Great Expectations* as she drove poor Pip to near insanity with her cold-heartedness.

Cherry has many of the traits women complain of in men: non-communicative, non-expressive of feeling except with her body, and exquisitely noncommittal. Emotionally unavailable, in the parlance of psychologists, she exemplifies the maddening contradictions that have made China source of my greatest sorrows and joys. As with my time at CRI or in my Leshan teaching job, I hung on in the hope that things might get better. But they never did.

I asked her once if the sex was just physical for her. Her answer was uncharacteristically emphatic and unequivocal: "My heart is in my vagina. I am not like some other girls who just have sex for the sake of it." So I was in her heart as well as her vagina? I cannot fathom this mystery.

Cherry also highlights the disproportionate desirability of young women in China. Unduly scarce due to China's policy of one child per family, they are accustomed to having the simultaneous attentions of several men. I can't tell you how many times I have been on dates with flirtatious females who finally revealed that they had a "boyfriend". Another consequence is that Chinese men exert stifling control and watchfulness over their women.

But in this battle of the sexes, men are not the victors. Dwain told me recently of a lover who showed up one day with a bruise on her face. Only then did she let him know about the jealous "boyfriend" who had caused it. And only when Dwain resolved to confront said "boyfriend" did the girl let him know that the aggrieved party was in fact her husband!

So lies are told, secrets kept, and jealousy is stoked. And I have noticed how casual the Chinese can be about lying. Not everyone, of course, but many. I recently discussed this with an elderly Chinese friend in London whose family had fled the Japanese invasion in the 1930s. He rued the loss of morality and courage from his race, attributing it to the Maoist era, when people had to lie and betray their friends and neighbors just to survive.

So I wonder what secrets Cherry is keeping? She told me once Western guys don't try as hard in pursuing women as Chinese guys. Well, whatever game I was meant to play, in the end I could not bear this slow death and dearth of a thousand cuts, the incremental starvation that leached life and love out of me, my essence ebbing away. Cherry savaged my joy, self-confidence, and peace of mind, almost tearing me from myself! It was an exasperating, exhausting endeavor, like Sisyphus pushing his rock up the hill, except worse in that this particular rock would frequently roll out of sight!

In the end, I had to acknowledge that, painful as it was to leave the relationship, it was even more so to stay in it!

Thirty-Three

So here I am in Beijing, weathering life's perfect triple storm: Sick, Loveless, and Broke!

Until recently, I was able to live a fairly comfortable life from doing voice recordings in Beijing. But it seems American accents are all the rage among Chinese educational publishers at the moment. And Brits like me and Bex and Cath have seen our work and revenue sources dry up.

So, after nearly two decades of exile — 14 years in New York City and five in China — I will return to the U.K., for fresh air if nothing else. Beijing is so toxic, with its construction dust, fumes, vehicle emissions, and factory effluent, and stressful, with its crowds and noise day and night.

I am tired of the dirty manners and discourtesies, the subway stink of garlic, farts, and body odor, taxi drivers who don't know their way round the city, and the subjugation of pedestrians by selfish drivers blaring their horns from shiny new German cars. This is not poverty of resources but of spirit!

As one of my friends lately advised me, "Enough is enough!" I must pack my bags, mission unfulfilled, "middle-aged, childless, and loveless" (to quote the closing moments of British television series *Brideshead Revisited*). China has got on my nerves long enough, literally *and* figuratively!

Perspectives From Peking

One

Fast-forward five years...

"Aliens shall not be employed in China without permission of the competent authorities of the Chinese Government." So says my airport arrival card for Beijing.

How do bureaucrats manage to make language so chilling, heartless, and bleak? I go to start a new job at China Central Television (CCTV). There have been occasional freelance jobs in Beijing since I left China in 2010, but this will be my first full-time assignment in the five years since.

"Competent"? I know only too well what counts for competence among Chinese state institutions. I saw it in my days as a teacher at corrupt universities, I saw it in the Chinglish scripts of Beijing publishers, and above all I saw it in the paranoid delusions of China Radio International.

What am I doing, going to this dust-swathed, mosquito-infested, dystopian metropolis, taking on full-time work and possible exhaustion, and leaving behind the spectacular beauty, gentle climes, and dear friends of West Sussex?

Money. Money. I need the bloody money! England withholds the financial backing that might empower me to enjoy its charms. Or do I go for Love? To dust off that tired old dream of finding a Chinese wife?

Perhaps the heart *does* have its reasons that Reason knows not of!

Two

"The mountains are bare and the rivers filthy. Sand and dirt rise up from the ground, and dust fills the sky." So said Choe Bu, a Korean official visiting Beijing in the 15th century. And as I look out of the hotel window at yet another rectangular concrete monstrosity, probably from the Soviet era, I am reminded of his words.

The great mythologist Joseph Campbell said that to understand a society, all you have to do is look at its biggest buildings and what they represent. What does this building in front of me declare? Inhuman, centralized, faceless power.

Well, the Chinese machine is not quite faceless. There's that tacky poster of Mao perpetually glowering over Tiananmen Square like some sulky granddad. And then there's the pretty woman in military uniform singing Chinese opera on the television sets inside each subway carriage. Product advertising follows, interspersed with images of smiling schoolchildren and footage of fearsome Chinese weaponry being paraded or test-fired. I just had an Orwellian moment!

It's all an expression of fear, as China's political elites patch up fragile egos craving impregnability, paranoia wrapped with color and noise, a puppet paper dragon pretending to be fierce. Revolution is merely having the courage to collectively state the obvious!

Anyway, there have been some pleasant surprises in my first few days this time in Beijing: that I will be doing cultural news at CCTV as opposed to business news, and that my daily start time is a civilized 11am, meaning I can ride reasonably uncrowded subways. I've even been told that the air quality in Beijing is improving. We'll see! Or not! Perhaps best of all, there is now a genuine and enforced smoking ban in indoor public spaces, including restaurants and bars. It came into effect just before I arrived!

The subway rides should also get shorter once I have moved closer to the new landmark CCTV building in the east of the city, where I will be working. However, I only have one month in hotel accommodation before I have to find and pay for an apartment. Landlords here expect three months' rent upfront in addition to the one-month security deposit, and I won't get my first paycheck until six weeks into the job. You do the math!

Have faith, Abdiel. It'll work out somehow. And after my year at CCTV is up, Sussex, Gloucestershire, Northumberland, and all the other places I have loved in England will still be there when I get back. Unless, of course, the fracking companies have got there first! Look after our Green and Pleasant Land, my fellow English!

Three

Thank God for Biteapitta, a restaurant serving Israeli food in the Sanlitun area. In a strange land of a strange language, strange customs, and strange food, do we not need a place of sanctuary where we are always welcome? Especially after my first foray into the staff canteen today at CCTV where, according to the translations, we were offered 'Oil with wormwood stalk' and 'white fungus soup'. I came away hungry!

And do we not need, to quote *Cheers*, a place "where everybody knows your name"? It is heartening, after my first day at CCTV, to be hailed as "YīngXióng" — my Chinese name, which means "Hero" — by staff who remember me from a year ago, when I was last here on a freelance assignment.

I am not sure what to make of the job yet: I have already seen some of my witty inventions replaced with dull verbiage. And I am "not insensible to these mutilations," to quote Thomas Jefferson.[47] But I try to remember that, like a stream flowing from an underground spring, though my output may be muddied, none can touch the source!

It's a distinction I could not make in the past, when I equated attacks, real or perceived, on my artistic output as attacks on me, as incremental destructions of my soul, reparable only by rebuke of the offending party with varying degrees of expletive-rich severity. That's a heavy burden to bear!

I have been assigned to the *Culture Express* show — with such riveting topics as thousand-dollar manicures and the world's longest pizza. The Chinese team members are voicing their own scripts, resulting in a litany of mispronunciation throughout the half-hour show.

At day's end, I met the show's glamorous Chinese-American host, Raquel Olsson. Gorgeous, probably married, probably already courted, wooed, and won by a favored suitor. And with a name like Olsson, her husband's probably some Nordic jock who rules among the financial elites during the week and sails a private yacht at weekends.

Still, her presence may redeem my trade in anodyne trivia from the base motive of paying bills to sacred offering on the altar of a screen goddess!

Four

Three days on the job, and things are on a more even keel. I suppose mood swings are inherent in such an abrupt change of life, and perhaps as time progresses, I shall transcend this emotional pendulum to reach transcendent detachment and equanimity.

I actually care about some of the stories I've been editing, such as a staging of *Macbeth* to open the Beijing International Theater Festival. And the treatment of my work has, on the whole, been respectful.

Having said that, one last-minute alteration by a Chinese overseer — or "laoshi" — goaded me to cross the floor and speak with him. I had quoted Shakespeare's "All the world's a stage" for a story about global online participation in recording *Yellow River Cantata*. Just before the show was to go on air, I noticed someone had changed the quote to "All the world *is* a stage"! What the fuck! Anyway, I managed to get the proper quote, and its iambic flow, restored.

After the show, I ran into that raven-haired heroine, Ms. Olsson, in the elevator. "Before I met you," I ventured, "I thought that with a name like Olsson, you would be blonde and Nordic."

"Oh, that's my husband's name," I expected her to reply. But instead she told me her father had Swedish ancestors "somewhere back several generations."

"Oh, so she's unmarried?" I pondered, as she got out on the tenth floor.

Five

Went to hear an evening of stand-up comedy by expats in the Gulou area. Top-quality stuff. Amazing how these guys, some of whom are just here for teaching assignments and never did stand-up before coming to China, have attained world-class standards!

To make Welsh jokes work in Beijing, which the English host Paul Creasy pulled off beautifully, is a feat of genius. He's one of those comedians who manages to be clever and funny at the same time. He went on to talk about the doctor who asked him if he was "comfortable" at the most intrusive moment of a medical exam, after which Creasy imagined offering an extended index finger to his houseguests with the words: "make yourself comfortable."

Another English comedian, Jon Matthews, thin, bearded, with long hair and baggy clothing, was hilarious on his physical similarity to conventional images of Jesus. It came about all because three guys in a bar one Christmas time had bought him free drinks with the quip, "Happy Birthday, man!" He dubbed them "The Three Wise Men".

The third Brit in the line-up, Nigel Tu, milked mirth in melancholia. Then there was a short, hairy American guy who described the night he was chatting up a girl in a bar before she went home with someone taller and better-looking. But then he imagined how the interloper would be jealously thinking about him later while in the act with her!

I've had some ideas of returning to the stand-up scene here myself, but after seeing such top-quality work, the idea is accompanied by a fair-sized dose of self-doubt.

Beijing enjoys an amazing wealth of creative talent in the English language: along with two stand-up nights a week, there's poetry, storytelling, and comedy improv. And then there are all the dance events, including Salsa, Swing, and Argentine Tango.

Beijing can be a playground for expat artists of every kind!

Six

It's an employee's market. A gathering of 40 of so people, mostly expats, falling over themselves to offer jobs! Someone needed a CEO for their operation, another sought a Beijing representative for their business. Design an app, join a team, run outdoor training camps, and so on.

The monthly event, entitled *Lean Startup Meetup*, is the brainchild of Rich Bishop, a Brit who has created a communal working space in the Liangmaqiao area. There's an infectious spirit of entrepreneurship here in Beijing, and a very real sense that anything is possible. A world away from the doom-filled corridors of London, I wonder if any of the foreigners here could have got their businesses underway, even allowed themselves to dream of them, in their home countries?

I have just gone on the accompanying website and come across an ad for a voiceover artist. Meanwhile, they're not using my voice much at CCTV's *Culture Express*. I gather the Chinese staff on the team have passed CCTV's internal certification for voiceover recording, meaning the scripts I have so meticulously prepared are mangled in the final broadcast. By and large, the narrations are delivered in thick Chinese accents replete with mispronunciation, sometimes downright incomprehensible and, to paraphrase Shakespeare, frighting English out of its wits.[48]

And Ms. Olsson, it turns out, who grew up in California, has the valley-girl vocabulary to match, so that 'tsars of Russia' becomes 'tars of Russia', Japanese 'incursions' are 'insertions', 'opulent' is 'oh-pulent', 'differs' 'de'fers', 'Narnia' 'Nar'near', and 'Carthage' 'Ca'tharge'! Oh dear, pedestal status revoked!

Seven

Things have gone well. I voiced a piece about the National Ballet of China performing at New York's Lincoln Center, and another on the *Soundscapes* installation at London's National Gallery. I requested these after adding Shakespeare references to both.

Meanwhile, I am to be a featured poet at an event in Beijing, this invitation coming after I shared some verses at an open mic. That kind of advancement never happened in England! The host of the evening, Matt Byrne, writes his own poetry in a style that reminds me of Dylan Thomas.

I have not come across a more creative, dynamic, engaged, imaginative, and above all confident group of people than the expats in Beijing. Perhaps we are all — to paraphrase Christ — prophets without honour in our home countries![49]

It's really only the money situation that's worrying me. I'm down to about £30 worth of RMB in the bank. Among the financial setbacks, some freelance teaching I was supposed to do this weekend got cancelled. Nor did I get the call, nor the returned call, to do some promised voice recording. And I am still awaiting payment for teaching a Tango class.

The root problem, though, is an employer who takes six weeks to make the first salary payment but only provides four weeks of accommodation!

Eight

I was almost in tears. This morning, over a cup of tea at the Xinhua news agency, Mr. Mi gave me an envelope with 2,000 RMB to help me through to payday next week. This because he knows I have to move out of the hotel tomorrow and don't have the money for alternative accommodation until I get paid.

That put a spring in my step! Earlier this week, I lamented to a friend in the U.K. that the world was refusing to provide the money I need to live, travel, and eat. But she divined "your vulnerability is your strength and point of connection" and that I would love to "live in the present and in full presence and receive presents!" How true her words proved!

Mr. Mi has long wanted me to work for Xinhua's television division — ever since I came in to voice a promo and narration for them several years ago. He says my insistence on crafting top-quality copy before doing the recording impressed him at the time. Since then, I have gone on to write and record several narrations for Xinhua documentaries and even given classes in voiceover to some of their anchors and other staff.

I would certainly have taken the job if Xinhua had made a competitive offer, but it too has structural inflexibilities built in. Mr. Mi doesn't let on about the internal machinations at work there, but I get the sense his efforts and standards are thwarted by higher-ups, and that they are struggling in a climate of perpetual reorganization and uncertainty.

Anyway, by the time I got back to the hotel this evening, I had received some payments owing. The hotel also agreed I could stay another week without a deposit and pay on checkout. Then one of my colleagues negotiated a lower room rate, and I received a voucher to further offset the final cost! Moreover, three other friends — two Chinese and one U.S. — also made offers of financial assistance after Mr. Mi's.

What a difference a day makes! Apparently, China *is* looking after me, and thanks be to God for the kindness of friends!

Nine

"Drink a lot of water!" That's the refrain I have heard countless times over the past week. I have come down with a severe case of what I call "Beijing Lung", and this is the suggestion nearly everyone makes.

Beijing's air has thickened of late into a permanent pale-grey smog or, as the government prefers to call it, "mist". The dust can also be intense, especially in subway corridors, which perpetually smell of cement. Meanwhile, Beijing is peppered with areas soaked in solvent fumes which must be neurotoxins.

Anyway, all these environmental assaults at once are a shock to the system, and my body has reacted. Consecutive nights of fever and piercing headaches have now resolved into a lingering cough and a sense of irritation from nose to throat to bronchial tubes to chest and lungs.

I go through this every time I come to Beijing. Everybody does. CCTV's guide book for new employees counsels, "It is not unusual to experience cold-like symptoms within a few days of arriving." And it advises, "Drink plenty of water." Got it, got it, got it. Drink plenty of water, and it will all get washed away!

Another well-meaning person today added her voice to the "drink-a-lot-of-water" chorus.

"I've drunk enough water to flood the plains of Sichuan!" I joked.

Perhaps the better advice would be: "Breathe less air"!

Ten

Never have I seen such an array of masculine beauty. It's why Homer could get away with calling the Greek warriors "the flower of manhood". A legion of tall, strapping, bare-chested foreigners wearing tight leather shorts, cross-strapped sandals, and long flowing cloaks at their backs assembled in Sanlitun.

But some saw not the sunset of that glorious day!

They had mustered for a promotional event. An establishment called 'Sweetie Salad' hired these "strong and handsome foreign models as a way to encourage our prospective customers to keep a healthy body shape." And they must have looked high and low to find this assembly of supremely conditioned lads among the foreigners of Beijing.

Unfortunately, Beijing's men in blue took exception to Sanlitun's lads in leather, and friends' photos posted on the social-media application WeChat show several police offers pinning down a couple of the leather-clad warriors on a nearby footbridge. Apparently, the presence of these so-called 'Spartans' caused such a commotion that some were arrested and dragged away for "affecting public order," whatever that means!

My own run-in with Beijing cops several years ago was a horrible ordeal, but I can only guess at the humiliation these lads must have endured sitting near naked on a cold bench in a police station. As *thebeijinger* magazine lamented, what began as "orderly formations at Guomao" ended in "tragic downfall on a bridge in Sanlitun."

Eleven

Progress on all fronts. I am established in a quiet, clean, comfortable apartment and, with the help of loans from friends, now repaid, taken on the high upfront costs. My landlord has also agreed to take three one-month payments of rent before three-month chunks kick in. My commute to work is pretty easy, and there's a cheap trolley service to the subway station.

Meanwhile, I have participated in several poetry evenings and enjoyed rapt audiences. The other day, I also attended a play reading with Beijing Playhouse — an expat-run organization putting on a few plays a year. Next up is *Table Manners*, for which I will audition in a few weeks.

Progress at work too, with more voicing of packages — as much as five on a couple of days in the half-hour program. That's not to say *Culture Express* is a high-quality show. Far from it. And Ms. Olsson, who left on "extended leave" never to return, has been replaced by a host with even worse delivery!

Nor are the hosts helped when their opening headlines are often drowned out by background noise and music, sometimes even by other voices talking in background clips! Duh! How can the production staff keep committing such basic and obvious errors?

Meanwhile, the show's repertoire of mispronunciation continues to gain new recruits: etiquette as "adequate", strudel as "struddle", antics as "antiques". There are horrors with names too —

Versailles as "Versells", W.B. Yeats as "W.B. Eats", and the pop group ABBA as "A-'BAH".

Despite such mutilations, I can at least maintain a high quality of the *written* word. Other than a few occasional injections of madness — such as altering my "Hilarity Ensues" in a headline to "Hilarity Ensures", the laoshis overseeing the texts are pretty much hands off.

In the past few weeks, World-War-II anniversary themes have dominated the show's agenda, with commemorative concerts, exhibitions, films, movies, etc., on repeating cycle. I'll be glad when the 3rd September celebrations have come and gone, because the repetition is very boring.

It's been 70 years since the conclusion of the "War of Resistance Against Japanese Aggression and World Victory Over Fascism". It's a long title Chinese officialdom has concocted, but then again, for the Chinese it was a very long war. World War II did not begin when Germany invaded Poland in 1939, but when Japan invaded China in 1937. Or even earlier, in 1931, if you include Japanese occupation in parts of the northeast.

Still, even with all the propaganda, China is not getting its main points across — either about its pivotal role in securing Allied victory, largely by forcing the Japanese military to divert resources from other theaters of conflict, or about the unhealed wounds of unacknowledged Japanese war crimes.

My Chinese colleagues don't seem to know much about their own history and, along with official commentators at every level, conflate China's war against the Japanese with the Communist Party's civil war against the Kuomintang Nationalist Party (KMT), which was suspended during World War II, in order to jointly resist the Japanese foe.

But, as the saying goes, "History is written by the victors," and CCTV scripts continue to praise the "revolutionaries" for their struggle against fascism, and Chinese people continue to believe — in the words of an elderly woman quoted on the BBC — that "It was Mao who defeated the Japanese." In reality, the KMT took far higher casualties in defending their country than did the Communists.

Meanwhile, I am managing to handle the undermining behavior of certain colleagues. An all too frequent pattern is to leave me with nothing to do for a couple of hours or more during the earlier part of the day and then pile in all the stories at the end, putting me under completely unnecessary pressure. At such times, team members have been urging me to press the 'Pass' button on stories I haven't even read!

It was gratifying, though, on one of these ill-structured days, to see the female director literally frogmarch away one of the team-members when he attempted to aggressively lecture me about the timing of stories. He's an annoying little shit, that one. Lazy too. Takes up space in scripts with empty words and repetition, and when I clean them up, complains that they're "too short."

Nor, the other day, could he be bothered to transcribe the soundbites in his stories, and when I asked him about it, he refused. I had to take a stand, reject his story, and tell the director. He finally remedied the gap, but now he's taking revenge by refusing to let me voice stories.

But he's no more than a mild irritation, a mosquito bite. And if I worked on another team, there'd be someone else just like him. May as well deal with the devil I know!

Twelve

Another trip down the Rabbit Hole today, September the Third. The *Culture Express* team were enlisted to cover Beijing's World-War-II 70th-Anniversary evening gala event, which followed the massive military parade earlier in the day. And they fucked it up royally!

How could a nation that demonstrates such lockstep precision among its marching ranks on the ground, and its squadrons of warplanes in the air, make such a dog's dinner of its television coverage in the evening?

The two live hosts were very poorly briefed on the subject matter and painfully ignorant about their nation's own history. Yet there they were improvising dialogue, speaking very slowly because they had nothing to say, and repeating themselves a dozen different ways.

Team preparation was pitiful too. At 6.20pm, a colleague came to me with three scripts, each with only a sentence or two, and asked me to add a few more paragraphs to each. "When do you need them by?" I asked. "6.30," she said. And it was complicated stuff, too — one about the 1937 Rape of Nanking by the Japanese military; another about eight Chinese women soldiers who drowned themselves in the Songhua River rather than surrender; and one about Japanese atrocities on prisoners of war.

For fuck's sake! They've had months to research and prepare all of this. Then they realize with minutes to go how thin their coverage is and call on me to produce a miracle! It's a marvel of incompetence, poor planning, and worse execution from start to finish. And though I have little experience as a TV presenter, surely I could do a more competent job — and certainly a better researched one — than those on air right now!

The control room for the recording studio was crammed with people during this fiasco, standing room only, but the output was all tin cans and string. I get the impression of a lost flock of sheep without a shepherd.

It was a fucking long day too. I was there until almost 10pm "just in case" I was needed, even though I had nothing to do after the show began at 6.30. And I was famished, having got to work that day only to discover that the staff canteen was closed, so that I ended up missing lunch.

But one upside of this Anniversary is all the blue-sky days we've had. The last time I saw the like was during the Beijing 2008 Olympics! The expats here are calling it "APEC-blue" after a run of clear days that occurred during the Asia-Pacific Economic Cooperation summit in November 2014.

Locals in Beijing are to be seen staring up incredulously at the now parted heavens, and wide vistas of blue dominate photos posted on WeChat. As one foreigner commented, "The weather is insanely nice and teases us for a brief moment about what Beijing could be if there was no corruption, coal consumption, or environmental degradation."

And we've had an especially long run of clear skies this time because the military parade followed Athletics World Championships that wrapped up last week in Beijing at the Bird's Nest Stadium. Hence the plea of Josh Tyas, one of Beijing's British stand-up comedians: "Come back, Usain. Usain Bolt! We need you! Beijing is surrounded by mountains! We'd never seen them before!"

Thirteen

Wealth, Wit, and Women. Well at least I've made some progress with the first two. Not that I can call my financial situation abundant yet, but it's nothing like as worrying as when I was last in the U.K.

Some potentially lucrative voiceover jobs fell through, though — one because they wanted a full-on American accent, another because they wanted a "deeper" voice. An animation project didn't materialize, and a corporate narration job was withdrawn after I corrected the Chinglish that riddled the script.

My only offsite jobs have been educational texts with dear Mr. Wang at Dawanglu. I used to do a lot of recordings for him when I last lived in Beijing, but the pay is pretty poor and hasn't gone up since I began in 2009. And it's a slow hard slog through hundreds of primary-school phrases — "The cat is on the chair" and the like — and I can only take a couple of hours of that in one go.

As for the Wit? I am a featured regular now at Poetry readings in Beijing. For my most recent outing at Mado Bar, I introduced a series about "courtship, love, sex, and genitals," and I'm happy to report my musings, wordplay, and double-meanings went down a treat.

Not sure about returning to stand-up, though that recent loss of a voiceover job to an American accent is certainly material, especially as the audiences here are mostly from the U.S. "Are there any Americans here tonight? ... Well, I don't mean to be racist, but ... have you listened to yourselves? Why do you talk like that?"

As for Women? Not much to report. The lovely 'Wing' suddenly showed up in Beijing last night for a business meeting she has today. Total surprise, and a welcome one. Ten years we have known each other, since we dated a few times at Chengdu University of Technology in my early teaching days in China. And we have remained in frequent contact since. I can't say that of anyone else I came to know all those years ago in Sichuan.

Wing does has a boyfriend, though, and she expects to get married next year. A generous reading of her predicament is that she is less than enthusiastic. But at the age of 30, she is being pressured by her family to settle down. She started to weep over dinner as she was telling me about it.

Outside, afterwards, we walked for a few minutes and I put my arm around her shoulders. She said something about an early start the next day and suddenly was waving to me from a taxi window! So we remain dear friends at opposite ends of the country.

Anyway, I then headed to Dongsishitiao for the closing moments of a Tango dance, or 'milonga'. Many slender beauties there in tight-fighting dresses. That's the second of two milongas I have attended now, and I will be taking several workshops this month. Romance has awakened for me in a dance studio before. I dare hope it may do so again.

Fourteen

Less than a week to go to the opening night of *Table Manners*, a play in Alan Ayckbourn's *Norman Conquests* trilogy, in which I am playing Norman. So much is riding on my performance, yet I feel a fraud sometimes. The smaller part of Tom was perhaps the more obvious casting choice.

The rest of the cast are really good too. So I don't have the small-minded comfort of "Oh, well at least I'm doing better than so-and-so." Everybody's bringing comedy to their roles, and everybody got off book quickly. There's no slacker in the cast on whom to pin my fragile ego.

I am especially impressed with Katja, who's playing my wife, Ruth, in her first-ever stage role and inhabiting the character just beautifully. And there's Kylie, an Australian girl, tall and pretty, and with the most alluring jade-like eyes, who is playing Annie. She hasn't been in a play since high school and is doing a wonderful job. It's humbling to see these relative newcomers take to their roles like fish to water. And disconcerting!

My performances in rehearsal have been hugely inconsistent, prompting the director, David Peck, to quip, "You're funny ... on a good day." It's a question of focus. When I embrace my overall motivation — David and I agreed on "I want to make you love me" — every comedic atom of the script dances with joy. But when I focus on "what am I doing with my hands?", the life drains out of my performance like a deflating balloon.

The great John Gielgud describes a similar affliction in his autobiography: "As soon as I began to think how I must walk and speak and act, I was paralyzed by self-consciousness and affectation ... I was acutely aware of my own graces and defects."

But when it came to playing Trofimov in Chekhov's *The Cherry Orchard* in 1924, "for the first time I looked in the glass and thought, 'I know how this man would speak and move and behave', and to my great surprise I found I was able to keep that picture in my mind throughout the action without my imagination deserting me for a moment."

I have been reinspired by Gielgud's realization that he could "live the part in my imagination." It's like the unbendable-arm exercise. Make a fist and crook your arm, with elbow by your side, so that your forearm is parallel to the floor. Ask a friend to try and force your fist up to your shoulder and try to resist them. Now do the same again, but instead of trying to resist them, pick a point on the wall and imagine a beam of light going from your fist to that point. Your arm becomes unbendable!

For me, "I want to make you love me" is one such point of light. In the end, perhaps this preoccupation with gestures, though it has dogged my acting for two decades, will prove a blessing in disguise. It requires me to hold some vision in my imagination that transcends all fear, doubt, and petty concerns. I also like to dance to the swing song, *Come On Be Happy*, as part of my warm-up. It brings out an energy and spirit suited to Norman's disposition.

Today, I'll put the word out to friends and contacts to come to the play. I've made every preparation possible, so it's time to release, trust, and embrace the moment.

So help me God.

Fifteen

"That's so Chinese!" It's a comment frequently heard in conversations between foreigners here in Beijing.

It was my turn to make this comment to Kylie, my fellow cast member on *Table Manners*, who until recently also worked at CCTV. She had met up for coffee with one of her former colleagues on the social-media team, who revealed that salary payments for Chinese staff on the team vary with the number of 'hits' they get on their stories. The colleague's own salary had been cut according to that criterion!

Kylie had wondered why so many fluff pieces — of the girls-skiing-in-bikinis variety — were making it on to the station's website. Now she knows!

Sixteen

Last night, our dress rehearsal for *Table Manners* was thoroughly dispiriting, but today, just in time for Opening Night, I finally found Norman's physicality — my shoulders somewhat slouched, knees slightly bent, a kind of nervous energy, and there he was!

Inhabiting that body, the whole part came so much easier. And just in time! Our first audience was a full house, and the laughs came throughout the show. Well done, everybody!

Seventeen

I'm fucking freezing! November the 2nd, and there's no heating! By government decree! Irrespective of what the thermometer is saying, buildings will not be heated until November the 15th!

I was cold throughout the night and now *have* a cold. I can only keep my apartment bearable by running the hot shower several times a day so that the place fills with steam!

Nor is the situation much better at work. Even after the 15th, they will keep the heating off on our floor, in order to "protect the machines" from overheating. I am in some dystopian nightmare here in China!

Anyway, my symptoms held off until completion of the *Table Manners* run. A very pleasing outcome on the whole. I flagged in the first act on Sunday, but the laughs were coming thick and fast in the second.

Meanwhile, no-one in the *Culture Express* team showed any interest in attending the show, even with the offer of comp tickets. A "dross of indifference," to quote D.H. Lawrence.[50] However, a couple of people from HR did come, as well as a Spanish colleague.

As our cast dinner wound up on Sunday night, Kylie of the jade green eyes reminded me we planned on going to a dumpling restaurant I told her of. To quote my rakish character of Norman in the play, I want to "make her happy." Offstage, however, I am more like the character Tom, in his doomed courtship of Kylie's character Annie, "missing the moment and kicking myself afterwards!"

Eighteen

Lies and false accusations again! I scored very high in my employee evaluation at CCTV, but then the leaders of *Culture Express* told HR they wanted to make a retrospective revision to the report!

The same day, they told me I must now come to work half an hour earlier than before and stay an hour-and-a-half later! Moreover, they now require me to sit in the frigid, overcrowded studio control room during broadcast, even though my work is done, in case of an "emergency".

I talked with Glen, the American HR person who recruited me in the first place. He too was baffled by the events of the day, by the sudden flurry of accusations, including fabrications that I had refused to edit stories and that I had taken too much sick leave.

Well, I have had two single days out sick in the five months since starting the job. I would probably have been better advised to stay out longer, but for knowing I am supposed to produce a doctor's note for anything more than a single day off work.

As for the accusation I refused to do my job, I can now trace it to a colleague's fury a week ago when I added contextual explanation before several Chinese idioms quoted in her script.

"It's not necessary!" she shouted.

"If we're going to quote someone using Chinese proverbs, they need some explanation," I replied.

Obviously on a very short fuse, she repeated her objection at even higher volume and stormed off.

I composed myself, put a note in the script that I was awaiting answers to queries, and got on with the rest of my job. Later, I noticed that someone had quietly removed the piece from the editing system. Yet somehow this was now grounds to argue I was refusing to do my job!

My adherence to decent standards has often met with resistance, but now it has inflamed a campaign of spite orchestrated by the two producers of *Culture Express*, a pair of mother hens who come in to work on alternate days. As the only foreigner on this particular team, I am highly exposed to their machinations.

Meanwhile, I don't know whether to be comforted or disturbed as I read *Wild Swans*, the family memoir so eloquently crafted by Jung Chang, in which she describes the climate of false accusation, fueled by personal vendetta, that destroyed so many lives during the so-called Cultural Revolution of the 1970s.

Will this, as Glen suggests, just "blow over"? Or is *Culture Express* undergoing a Cultural Revolution of its own?!

Nineteen

I hope I'm not going to get someone killed with my fraudulent behavior today.

Mr. Wang, who runs his independent recording studio near Dawanglu, asked me to voice a script for him about "pertrochanteric fractures", "intertrochanteric fractures", "extended subtrochanteric fractures", and "ipsilateral femoral shaft fractures".

Then followed a dizzying array of ungrammatical instructions and lists of scary instruments — nails, pins, screws, wrenches, blades, and drill bits "to drill through both cortex" — apparently to guide surgeons using a manufacturer's equipment, but rather invoking images of Dantesque tortures!

Mr. Wang informs me the script was likely translated by local students. Hence, as so often happens in China, cheap instructions accompany expensive equipment!

I'm such a whore for making this recording! I should refuse to gild this garbage with my voice, but I desperately need the money as I limp to the next paycheck. Difficult days.

Twenty

"We frequently spent ten hours in the fields doing a job which could have been done in five. But we had to be out there for ten hours for it to be counted as a full day."

As I continue reading *Wild Swans*, I am struck by the echoes of the Cultural Revolution at work. I have had two hours arbitrarily added to each workday by the two-faced matriarchy in charge of this show.

The fact that I always have the day's work requirement thoroughly and comfortably completed to the highest standard in the original timeframe, is irrelevant. Now, I must suddenly be here for the extra hours to meet unspecified "regulations". And, as repeated in an email setting out "requirements as requested," whatever that means, I must be in the control room during broadcasts, even though my work is completed beforehand.

Nor is there any regard for the editing I am sometimes called to do from home, nor the hours of my own time spent researching topics relevant to the show. (I posted links to these resources on the *Culture Express* WeChat group, though no-one paid the slightest attention.)

The hypocrisy is rampant. The matriarchs typically take lunch breaks exceeding two hours, compared to my 30 minutes. They also alternate their days at work, so that each is out of the office for more than half a year. Yet they complain that I have had two sickdays thus far!

As one of my foreign colleagues on the same floor astutely observes, *Culture Express* is "too many chiefs and not enough Indians." Too true. Producing nothing of value in their own lives, they have made it their mission to interfere with mine!

Meanwhile, their justifications are becoming increasingly ludicrous. I should be there during the broadcast, they say, "in case there are spelling mistakes in the titles." But of course, I have already spell-checked every single piece prepared for the line-up well before the show goes on air, nor have I ever made an error!

Then their fall-back reason is "in case there are mispronunciations during the broadcast!" It's a live show, for fuck's sake! The hosts' mispronunciations are legion, despite my best efforts to forestall them — even coaching them where possible beforehand — but I don't have a fucking time machine to travel back and redeem their incompetence!

I talked about all this with a friend in the U.K. last night. She pointed to the "web of domination" at work in China, that the experience at CCTV is part of the same culture that tells people when, or if, they can have heating in their homes or offices.

Until last week, I was content, motivated, and enjoying a good life-work balance that allowed me to rehearse for a play and avoid the worst of Beijing's subway crush. But living a life I love is obviously deeply offensive to others!

Twenty-One

I went to the hospital this morning after waking in the middle of the night with tightness and pain in my chest, something I have never experienced before. I returned to CCTV with a doctor's certificate specifying I should have rest and not undergo stress.

How did Matriarch Two respond? By moderating my hours? No! She stood up, filed the paper in a drawer, and said, "I think you do too much theatre!"

"Excuse me for having a life!" I replied.

Twenty-Two

I'm facing a hydra at CCTV! And she has just grown an extra head! This time, it's the head of HR, a third matriarch, mouthing the incantation, "regulations must be followed!"

People now in positions of authority in China grew up during the Cultural Revolution, and patterns of rigidity are hardwired into their DNA. But look back in China's history, and it has always been a highly centralized, top-down regime. I share the frustrations of Tang-Dynasty poets Li Bai and Du Fu, who spoke out against the imperial system and were punished as a result.

That's the pattern at work here, and it isn't Communism. Communism died in China in the 1940s to be supplanted by Mao's paranoia that hounded to death the very idealists who had sacrificed so much to install him!

Just as the word "Democracy" is, to quote Arundhati Roy, "the Free World's whore, willing to dress up, dress down...",[51] the word "Communism" performs the same service for China! Both are convenient veneers for abuse of power, paranoia, and control!

And the result at CCTV is to create a vampiric monster sucking the lifeblood and joy out of this China experiment. Fuck this!

Twenty-Three

The next experience inspired a poem, which I here allow to speak for itself. A word of explanation first: "san san yao" means the number "331", and "san yao yao" means "311".

Miss Spent

A call-girl called at my door today
Or so I suppose she was -
A little pink skirt though it's snowing outside
And more confirmed because

She had a suitcase by her side,
I wonder what tricks within?
Should I pretend to be whom she sought
And could that be a sin?

But caught unawares in a disheveled state
In my jammies at two o'clock,
Nonplussed by the lovely mirage lent by fate,
Thought lagged the awakening cock.

Our foreign languages misunderstood,
She phoned and was told "san san yao."
A neighbor it was, and I missed a digit:
My apartment is just san yao yao!

Perhaps when her client is finished,
The other had his fun,
She might return to make good on her error,
With two for the price of one!

> Nov. 22, 2015

Twenty-Four

Screen-tested for an anchor position at CCTV. I would give myself 8 out of 10. Don't know how I came across on camera. I was so tired that my left eye was partly occluded. This followed a night of headaches after a CT heartscan the previous day. I can still taste the iodine, used as a contrast medium, injected before the scan.

The screentest comprised reading from teleprompter, relatively easy, followed by responding, unbriefed, to a breaking news item from recent events. They chose the terrorist attacks in Paris, and I interviewed a pretend commentator as if in real time.

Since doing the test, I have heard some whisperings from "l'esprit d'escalier". Why didn't I ask more challenging questions? What about the fumble as footage ran? Was I gesturing too much during the reading? Was I squared up to the camera or slightly oblique to it?

Anyway, whatever the outcome, I have asked for a copy of the video to assist with my own development and learning. In the meantime, let's see if CCTV regards me worthy of admission into its ranks of on-air mediocrity.

Twenty-Five

Saw the video of my screentest for the Anchor position. Not bad. But I did look tired and stressed. The daily grinding burden here is writ large. This job is as salt that has lost its savor, to paraphrase Christ's simile, and that savor can never be regained.[52] Meanwhile, the words of Jung Chang in *Wild Swans* continue to sound their melancholy and all too familiar note:

> *I found this environment unbearable. I could understand ignorance, but I could not accept its glorification, still less its right to rule.*

And now, the environment outside the building is almost as poisonous as that within! Foreign friends are calling it the "air-pocalypse". Surrounding the windows of the 38th floor, even at noon, is a toxic milky pall, the colour of illness, the colour of death. The particle readings now are off the scale — in technical speak, PM 2.5 levels exceeding 2,200, compared with a World Health Organisation safety level up to 25!

We are living in a smog phantom. But don't worry. China has just told the world it has met its pollution-reduction targets!

Twenty-Six

Joyous times at my apartment with dear friends on Boxing Day. This was my Christmas celebration as I, along with most of my foreign colleagues at CCTV, had to work on Christmas Day, which fell on a Friday.

Laughter, banter, and charades into the early hours. And, thanks to the first and newly opened Marks & Spencer in Beijing, I was able to provide Christmas pudding, mince pies, and even brandy butter in true British tradition!

Dance friends "Brother Herman" and his partner Mei were there, bringing a selection of my favourite Western cakes; Paul, a Brit, came with his Chinese wife Judy, and contributed a home-made Christmas pud of his own; Bill, another Brit who works at CCTV, came with his wife Gwen; my Canadian neighbour Wendy made a fabulous mulled wine; Eugénie, the French costume designer for *Table Manners* came, as did "Brother Dwain", whom I have known for several years since we were both teachers in Changping. He is in Beijing for a few weeks before returning to L.A. to resume his flourishing screenwriting career.

And, most memorably for me, Jessica. As she and I went to retrieve her coat from my bedroom, our foreheads touched, a tender kiss on the lips.

Who is Jessica? A long-limbed Chinese beauty I first met a couple of summers ago in a maze of Beijing alleys — or "hutongs" — as we were separately searching for the same event. We stayed in touch, but a couple of months ago, on a very crowded morning subway train, I got a WeChat message from her, asking if I was standing by the door. As I looked around, she was making her way through the throng towards me.

Was this what the Chinese call "Yuanfen" — a word meaning something like "fate" or "destiny" and often applied to couples?

Since then, Jessica has joined me for several events, including stand-up comedy, improv shows, and my own poetry evenings. At the most recent one, in Mado Bar, I shared the following sonnet. I did not name Jessica as my muse to the audience, but she knew it was about her. And though she likely wasn't clued in to the double-meanings of my last six lines, the poem had some effect, for we had a lovely cuddle in the taxi afterwards.

Ode to Jessica

Lost in the labyrinth, we wanderers found
Each other, then more recently again,
While kept in crowded transit underground,
Journeys coincident confirmed Yuanfen.
Then we in theatres laughter exchanged
Where improvisers, travelling realms absurd,
Invented in their frenzy near deranged,
As lunatics and poets dwell on a word.
We then were side by side, but now I stand
Performing to delight you in the stall,
Embodiment concluded by your hand
And bow before you as the curtain fall.
This is our journey's end, each in our role,
Combining parts to make a perfect whole!

Twenty-Seven

I received a formal warning today because, for the past week, I left work when finished, rather than staying on to sit through the show's airing. The matriarchs noted my absence and reported it to HR, who in turn have emailed me to say "punishment will be imposed accordingly."

So now at 2am, I am weighing my options. Quitting the job is tricky, as the visa is tied to it. Meanwhile, rent's due yesterday, and I am expecting my next salary payment within days.

Meanwhile, nothing is moving in my life. Because of the job, I am too tired to get out to Tango events and the other things I love in Beijing, and I am finishing the workdays too late to be available for freelance work. No progress in love, either, just enough money to cover things but no surplus, no pathway I can see to publishers for my many writings, and no acting.

I can barely muster the enthusiasm even to write this entry. Sometimes, I just wanna get off this fucking planet!

Twenty-Eight

Today, I get a Second Warning Letter from HR! And all because I was out sick today! In a litany of lies, it accuses me of being "absent without notification." But not only did I inform the relevant matriarch in plenty of time I wasn't going to make it in today, I even offered to do the work from home instead!

She sent a message refusing that offer so, according to established procedure, I checked with the news room that provides coverage, confirmed that they could cover, informed her, and that should have been the end of it.

But the same afternoon, in comes this threatening email. When I called HR, they told me, "if you could offer to work at home, you could work at the office." Hell no, I couldn't! Tower 2 is no place to be when you're sick, where people have to wear hats and coats all day long because the building is unheated! And temperatures outside are now falling below minus 15 Celsius!

It isn't easy staying well in these conditions, huddled in hoodie and coat, coughing my way through the days while a ventilation fan blows cold air at the back of my head, and surrounded by a chorus of coughing from others similarly bundled in their layers. Even as someone who takes care of himself, practises yoga daily, and never smokes, I have incubated a relentless cough for months now!

To top it all, none of the foreign staff have yet received our salary for the month. I checked with HR and was told it will arrive a week after the due date! We weren't even notified of this! What's more, a new tax is going to be levied against our salaries! Backdated to last month!

I would quit if I weren't so strapped for money! Why does life come down to this?

Twenty-Nine

The level of malice is staggering! The CCTV chiefs have not only fined me for the day I was out sick — combining this with the outright lie that I had failed to notify them — but have now retrospectively levied another fine for another day I was out sick several weeks ago. And these are only the third and fourth days of sickness I have had in eight months!

Both fines — each exceeding a day's pay — are on the grounds I did not produce a doctor's note, when in fact I had been told on my very first day of employment that I did not *need* to do so for a single day! Nice little trap laid for me there!

I did, however, get a doctor's note recommending I take five days of rest. What I got in response was permission to leave an hour earlier for the remainder of the week. But even this was grounds for HR to accuse me of "leaving your workstation early," as if it had not been sanctioned.

All of this has been orchestrated between *Culture Express* Matriarch One and her friend and head of HR, Liye, whose name is a suitable homonym for her character! In short, one head of this hydra is spitting out lies, and the other is putting her official stamp on them!

One of the kinder team members on *Culture Express* told me there have been many copy editors before me who were deeply unhappy there. I can relate! This situation may be even worse than CRI! And that's going some! Not content with sapping my energy, such that I limp home at the end of the week too tired and sick even to go out, now this vampiric monster wants to eat my very bones!

Thirty

"It's not easy to properly reject you."

Fuck! Was ever a more devastating line delivered from beloved to lover? Well, it was Jessica's line to me over WeChat. She was supposed to let me know if she'd join me for a dance event, but then failed either to show up or inform me! When I complained, this was her response! Good to know where I stand, I suppose!

And last night I went out with Camilla, one of those head-turning classic Chinese beauties. It was a third date and followed a very amorous evening in Chaoyang Park a couple of weeks ago. Cut a long story short, she has decided to remain with the person she was already seeing, whose existence I discovered when our walk to the subway was interrupted by his call to her mobile phone!

And it turned cold last night literally as well as metaphorically. I gallantly put my nice warm coat over Camilla on this uncharacteristically chilly April night, for she had come out in summer attire, and got sick myself as a result! I didn't get the girl, but at least I caught a cold!

I feel fucking useless and undesirable. Nothing is working out at any level. No one to love, no employment lined up for when my contract with CCTV expires in June, and precious few sales of my newly published epic poem, *Obama's Dream*. So much for my dream of being a writer, let alone an actor!

It really feels like there's no hope, no point in trying, no point in going on. What am I doing here on this earth? It's all so fucking pointless. Every single prospect vanishes before my eyes. What have I done to deserve this punishment of Tantalus?

If things don't work out in a relationship or a country, don't we leave it? Then why not leave this world?!

Thirty-One

A bit of magic over the weekend. I recently met a theatre producer looking for a project, who asked me what plays I would like to be in. I gave her a list of several suggestions, including *The Dresser*, as well as plays I'd love to redo, such as *Orphans*, the intense and gritty three-hander in which I played Harold back in 2009 at my beloved Penghao Theatre.

It was to *Orphans* that her heart responded. Meanwhile, Mr. Wang, owner of Penghao, has adored the play ever since we staged it, continually sings the praises of our production, and lauds my performance every time I revisit the theatre.

I arranged a meeting at the theatre with the producer, along with Peter Walters, director of the previous incarnation. Mr. Wang happened to be in that day, and we all agreed to a re-run!

Sometimes, doubt creeps in about whether I can replicate my accomplishments of several years ago, but then I recall actor Antony Sher's observation in his autobiography *Beside Myself*, that the best advice for an actor is to say "fuck it!"

So fuck it! It's on!

Thirty-Two

I have written a script for a three-minute video that sets out China's claims to the islands in the South China Sea. From a historical perspective, China has a point. The islands were settled by Chinese people over a thousand years ago, and the famed admiral Zheng He swept the area clean of pirates some 600 years ago.

This was for a freelance job I was given at the weekend. But the simple, powerful, and effective text I lovingly crafted has been replaced by an ugly monstrosity of Chinglish replete with spelling, grammatical, and formatting horrors — one that attempts to get in "all the information." That means every minute detail, relevant or irrelevant, about dates, dynasties, maps, and numbers of ships and crew.

All this would serve in a half-hour documentary, but rips apart any chance of coherence in a three-minute video! And worse, the script requires speed-reading to get through in time! Now, my job is to "polish" this turd!

Thirty-Three

David Crook is a fascinating character. Born in 1910, he went through careers as a journalist, activist, and Communist spy. But for most of his life, he served China as an English teacher, laying the groundwork, together with his wife Isabel, for what is today Beijing Foreign Studies University (BFSU).

And it was at the BFSU theatre — in an evening themed "China-UK in Drama" — that I embodied David on stage, recreating the moment in 1948, in a village called Shilidian, that the couple decided to remain in the country and serve as teachers.

It was also wonderful to see, going on before us, a cross-dress Chinese version of *A Midsummer Night's Dream*. Their excerpt included a very glamorous male Titania who evoked riotous laughter among the largely Chinese audience.

And, to cap it all, Isabel Crook, David's widow, now approaching her 102nd birthday, was in the audience and joined us on stage at the end!

Thirty-Four

"Unloved, unmourned, and alone," I thought to myself as I left the control room on Friday evening, my last day at CCTV. But then I heard someone call my name. I turned round to see Chloë, one of the *Culture Express* team.

"I heard today's your last day," she said.

I don't recall much of the following conversation, but I treasure her tears, which welled up as we talked and overflowed, despite her best efforts to contain them.

I am deeply moved to realize I am missed by at least one member of the team. I gave Chloë a hug and told her she had been as a sister to me. For, on the occasions I voiced her stories, we exchanged brief moments of conversation, discussing such topics as the Chinese science-fiction writer Liu Cixin, of whom she is also a fan.

Then several others of the team came out, and I embraced them too. Among them was Shen Li, who studied in Paris and with whom I used to discuss Chinese novelist and Nobel laureate Mo Yan; and Li Xiang, one of the first to buy my book *Obama's Dream* and among the audience at a recent book talk I gave.

I will also miss the new host for *Culture Express*, Jennifer Hsiung. With her background in theatre and stand-up comedy, finally the show has a presenter who can articulate a clear sentence in English!

The affectionate farewells imparted a happy ending to this dismal year at CCTV. I wonder what motivated the matriarchs' campaign of hatred and persecution, the lies and slanders, the arbitrary abuse of power, the fines for getting sick in a sick building? Was it gender politics against a man in a largely female team? Was it racism against the only foreigner? Was it my audacity in pursuing a creative life outside of work? Was it for shining too bright in a dark cage, or my insistence on high standards?

Perhaps all of the above. In the end, my year at CCTV was one of treasured sisters and contemptible mothers. It is, of course, futile trying to untangle "the mystery of iniquity"[53] motivating these malevolent matriarchs, but my very existence seemed to provoke their most malicious impulses!

Still, Fortune handed me a gift when I came to work on Tuesday. In one of the most disingenuous pleasantries I have ever heard, Matriarch One said "Morning" to me as I walked past. I very publicly blanked her and just kept walking!

So I close out this latest year in China with a mixed review — some theatrical success, a blaze of poetry, certainly a year of producing excellent scripts and narration at CCTV, but also a long, depressing, and dismal grind, when I was robbed of time and energy to do the things I love, robbed of joy, robbed of my lifeforce or, as Jennifer quipped in one of our frequent conversations on the culture of *Culture*, robbed of my mojo!

So thank you, Chloë, for your parting gift, a sweet dessert after this bitter pill. Are not your tears listed in Heaven's scroll?[54] Certainly, they are lovingly writ in my memory. And farewell, my dear sisters on *Culture Express*.

Thirty-Five

In the end, I couldn't get out of China fast enough! In May, the apartment building where I live, formerly a hotel, cranked up the central air-conditioning system to such an infernal pitch that the vibrations rocked the floor, walls, ceilings, and even the headboard of the bed where I was trying to sleep!

And none of the messages, phonecalls, and interventions of bilingual friends — whether to the apartment owner, lettings agent, or building management — did anything to alleviate the situation.

When I first complained, management said they'd take a look at the air-conditioning in my room. I tried to explain that the noise was not coming from my room; the source was the central system in the basement below.

"We'll look at your room," they repeated.

"But the problem's not *in* my room. The noise is still there when my own air-conditioning is turned off!"

It took me 10 days just to get them to acknowledge that much. I even took one of the managers down there to hear for himself. It's like being in the engine room of an enormous ship that sounds like it's about to blow up at any moment!

"Please reset the system to its levels last summer," I conveyed. "When I first moved into the building, there was no problem!"

They responded by saying they'd install soundproofing. That wouldn't do any good when the whole structure of the building is vibrating! Then they said they'd get their engineers to take a look. Then they said they'd order a part to replace what was at fault, that it would arrive after the Dragon-Boat-Festival holiday. The festival came and went. Nothing changed over an entire month!

While all this was going on, I hoped at least to manage some afternoon naps in the two weeks of holiday I had saved up to the end of my contract with CCTV. But even that was denied. About a week after the air-conditioning went into overdrive, they started ripping out the building's second floor — just below me on the third — dragging out heavy equipment and furniture from disused conference rooms and catering facilities, down the neighbouring stairwell and lift shaft, scraping it across the concrete of the building's front lot, and hauling it onto several waiting lorries.

This would go on all day, starting at 7am, Saturdays and Sundays included! And when they finished that, they followed up with the constant din of jackhammers, saws, drills, and banging right below me.

Then I realized there is *also* major construction underway on the building's *top* floor, the 16th, which, with its deep rubble and piles of rubbish, looks like the aftermath of a nuclear holocaust! Again, the stairwell and lift shaft right beside my apartment are the main point of access for this crew!

All this highlights the selfish disregard for others' quality of life that prevails throughout mainland China. Just about every foreigner I have met in Beijing has experienced difficulty sleeping because of construction noise at all hours of the day and night. Even my German friend, nestled in the relative comfort of a German-embassy apartment complex, has had to endure round-the-clock construction work from a new building going up next door, complete with deliveries of supplies and equipment through the night.

Luckily, my landlord took responsibility and allowed me to leave my contract a month early with full refund of the last month's rent and deposit.

So now I'm headed back to Argentina, after an absence of 11 years. But that's another story…

Closure

I once saw a featherless parrot, caged in a friend's house in California. My friend explained that the bird was a rescue, that it had been so psychologically traumatized in its former home that it continued to self-harm by plucking its own feathers!

I often return to this image in trying to understand China's psychological condition. The genocide and civil war that ravaged the nation in the first half of the 20th century were followed by *self-inflicted* genocide and famine under Mao, whose 'Cultural Revolution' instilled a fear-based motivation polluting the nation's subconscious to this day.

And from this poisoned source springs the society's "web of domination", its "culture of impunity", "loss of morality and courage", and the spiritual impoverishment bemoaned in this book. Human beings are commoditized, quality of life is outlawed, and paranoia cloaked in the flag of Communism. Meanwhile, China continues to "grow faster than its competence."

Similar observations are expressed by Beijing Playhouse theatre impresario Chris Verrill, who staged the *Table Manners* production in which I played Norman. In his farewell video of March 2018, having lived in China for 13 years and "thrown in the towel" after the government finally suffocated his Playhouse to death, he says:

> *It has been an adventure, a lot of it very good, a lot of it very bad... To all my friends back in America and around the world who fear China becoming the next world superpower, you have nothing to worry about. China looks big and strong on the outside, but it is a very fragile house of cards, and it will implode...*

"It has been an adventure, a lot of it very good, a lot of it very bad..." My sentiments exactly! Perhaps the most consistent theme of this book is China's extreme contrasts, reflected in my own rollercoaster ride between delight and despair, reverie and revulsion, reeling in a nation of kind hearts but with "fiends in the workplace!"

Westerners who elect to live and work in China may find themselves undergoing similar mood swings. For them, I hope this book will steady the ride. Others I bid enjoy the sound and fury[55] from a safe distance. For my own part, I am completing this book on the far side of the globe!

About the Author

Thank you for purchasing this book, and if you enjoyed it, do leave a kind review at Amazon US or Amazon UK. Abdiel's non-fiction publications also include *The Gourmet Gospel: A Spiritual Path to Guilt-Free Eating*.

Abdiel's themes are deeply informed by Shakespeare, the Bible, and mythological sources, especially in his epic poems. In 2016, he published the "little epic", *Obama's Dream*, taking the former president on a shamanic journey of transformation while exposing the violations of empire handed over to Donald Trump. Go to Abdiel's website at poetprophet.com/Contact to get a FREE copy of this book as well as a sample of his signature epic poem, *Elijah*.

Meanwhile, Abdiel's poetry collections include his three-volume *Verses Versus Empire* series, covering in turn the Bush, Obama, and Trump eras; and *Well Versed: To Shakespeare, Poets, and the Performing Arts*, featuring poems narrated in BBC broadcasts by famed British actors, among them Mark Rylance, Kenneth Branagh, and Judi Dench. Finally, he has written a novella for children entitled *The Christmas Tree*.

Abdiel's own skills as a narrator, including a wide range of characters and accents, make for lively and dramatic readings. You can hear audio excerpts from all his books at poetprophet.com.

Before coming to China in 2005, Abdiel worked as a journalist in London and New York for the Reuters news agency, where his reporting ranged from currency-market analysis to Biblical scholarship. Later, he wrote articles and press releases on commercial insurance for Standard & Poor's. His passions include Argentine Tango, Yoga, and competitive Swimming.

Author website: poetprophet.com

Contact the Author

poetprophet.com/contact

Footnotes

1. *Hamlet*, II.ii.

2. China Central Television (CCTV) has since been rebranded as China Global Television Network (CGTN).

3. *Richard III*, I.ii.

4. Shakespeare, *1 Henry IV*, I.iii.

5. Psalm 42:7.

6. Matthew 16:25.

7. 2 Timothy 1:6.

8. From *Oliver Twist*.

9. A phrase borrowed from D.H. Lawrence's poem, *Last Lesson in the Afternoon*.

10. Matthew 13:3-7.

11. 2 Corinthians 6:14.

12. Matthew 7:6.

13. Proverbs 4:23.

14. 2 Corinthians 11:14.

15. Matthew 23:24.

16. Isaiah 5:20.

17. Mark 3:1-5.
18. 1 Kings 19:4.
19. Romans 10:6-7.
20. Exodus 5:6-9.
21. Shakespeare, *Pericles*, V.i.
22. Titus 2:15.
23. 1 Corinthians 9:19-20.
24. From his poem, *Last Lesson of the Afternoon*.
25. *The Merchant of Venice*, I.iii.
26. Matthew 10:16.
27. Shakespeare, *Henry V*, II.ii.
28. Psalm 18:1-19.
29. Genesis 4:12.
30. Shakespeare, *A Midsummer Night's Dream*, III.ii.
31. Matthew 13:58; Mark 6:5.
32. Proverbs 29:18.
33. Deuteronomy 30:19.
34. Matthew 7:24-27.

35 Shakespeare, *Hamlet*, III.ii.

36 Hata was briefly Japan's prime minister in 1994 after breaking with the Liberal Democratic Party whom he accused of corruption.

37 This use of the term "revolutionary" to describe China's resistance against Japanese invaders during World War II is false and misleading, as it suggests victory was entirely a Communist-Party achievement. I examine this phenomenon more closely in *Perspectives From Peking*, Chapter 11.

38 Matthew 23:24.

39 Exodus 9:1.

40 1 Chronicles 16:22; Psalm 105:15.

41 Team GB's rankings went on to rally even further, to third place in the medal standings in London (2012), and second in Rio (2016), where "we" surpassed China!

42 Matthew 6:28-29.

43 Malachi 3:16; Luke 10:20; Philippians 4:3; Revelation 3:5.

44 John 5:1-9.

45 Shakespeare, *The Merchant of Venice*, III.i.

46 Shakespeare, *Othello*, II.iii.

47 As a Congressional committee was editing his draft for *The Declaration of Independence*.

48 *The Merry Wives of Windsor*, II.i.

49 Mark 6:4.

50 From his poem *Last Lesson of the Afternoon*.

51 In her speech of May 13, 2003 at the Centre for Economic and Social Rights in New York, Roy said:

> *Every kind of outrage is being committed in the name of Democracy. It has become little more than a hollow word, a pretty shell, empty of all content or meaning. It can be whatever you want it to be. Democracy is the Free World's whore, willing to dress up, dress down, willing to satisfy a whole range of tastes, available to be used and abused at will.*

52 Matthew 5:13.

53 2 Thessalonians 2:7.

54 Psalm 56:8.

55 Shakespeare, *Macbeth*, V.v.

Made in the USA
San Bernardino, CA
25 March 2018